WE ARE
HR

THE BUSINESS OWNER'S DEFINITIVE GUIDE TO
PROFESSIONAL EMPLOYER ORGANIZATIONS

WE ARE
HR

BILL J. LYONS

ForbesBooks

Published by ForbesBooks, Charleston, South Carolina.
Member of Advantage Media Group.

ForbesBooks is a registered trademark, and the ForbesBooks colophon is a trademark of Forbes Media, LLC.

Printed in the United States of America.

10 9 8 7 6 5 4 3 2 1

ISBN: 978-1-95086-318-1
LCCN: 2020922513

Cover design by David Taylor.
Layout design by Mary Hamilton.

This custom publication is intended to provide accurate information and the opinions of the author in regard to the subject matter covered. It is sold with the understanding that the publisher, Advantage|ForbesBooks, is not engaged in rendering legal, financial, or professional services of any kind. If legal advice or other expert assistance is required, the reader is advised to seek the services of a competent professional.

Advantage Media Group is proud to be a part of the Tree Neutral® program. Tree Neutral offsets the number of trees consumed in the production and printing of this book by taking proactive steps such as planting trees in direct proportion to the number of trees used to print books. To learn more about Tree Neutral, please visit **www.treeneutral.com**.

Since 1917, Forbes has remained steadfast in its mission to serve as the defining voice of entrepreneurial capitalism. ForbesBooks, launched in 2016 through a partnership with Advantage Media Group, furthers that aim by helping business and thought leaders bring their stories, passion, and knowledge to the forefront in custom books. Opinions expressed by ForbesBooks authors are their own. To be considered for publication, please visit **www.forbesbooks.com**.

This book is dedicated to the incredibly talented team of professionals at Lyons HR, who inspire me every day, and to my business partners Bruce Cornutt, Alan Ridgway, Ginger Bateman, Jeanny Williams, Catherine Harper, Wade Krett, Marty Abroms, and Brad Buttermore, whose wisdom and counsel have been instrumental in our growth and success.

CONTENTS

ACKNOWLEDGMENTS

Sitting prominently on a bookshelf in my office is a plaque that reads, "There is no limit to what a man can do or where he can go if he doesn't mind who gets the credit." This famous quote by Ronald Reagan reminds me every day to appreciate the people I've leaned on for support over the years, and it reminds me that success is a team effort. Anyone who leads an organization knows that success or failure depends largely on the people around you—people who not only are knowledgeable, competent, and skilled but who also possess the kind of positive attitude that lifts morale and inspires everyone to achieve greater heights. These are the people I have the privilege of working with every day. Lyons HR would not exist, nor would this book be possible without them.

I want to thank my parents, Bill and Tillie Lyons, who for over sixty years have taught me the importance of remaining committed to something you believe in. My dad instilled within me a strong work ethic and impressed upon me the importance of having integrity in everything you do. He is the product of a generation that believes your word is your bond—that when you shake a man's hand, you've given your word, and that's something you just never break. My mother was the epitome of unconditional love. Never concerned about material things, she taught me how to be compassionate and empathetic and how to treat other people. She used to tell me that people may forget what you say, but they will never forget how you make them feel. Chapter seven of this book, "Culture Creators," is heavily influenced by lessons I learned from my mother.

There are many professionals in the PEO industry who have been around longer than me and who know more than I do. But if there is one area in which I excel, it's asking good questions. I learned very early in my career when to talk and when to listen (with emphasis on the latter). I discovered that learning occurs when you seek the advice of people who know more than you do. When we started our PEO, no one was more helpful or influential than Dan McHenry. From our first introduction, Dan has been a trusted advisor, guiding us through the early formation of our PEO and helping us develop meaningful operational processes and metrics, which continue to serve us to this day. Dan is a giant in this industry, and I am proud to call him my friend.

I want to thank every client of Lyons HR—past, present, and future—who entrusts us with the welfare of their most valuable asset, their people. And a special thanks to Mr. Jim Spinks, who took a chance on a start-up PEO all those years ago. Jim was one of our first clients, and there was no way I was going to disappoint him. The partnership we forged at the beginning remains strong to this day.

Finally, I want to thank my loving wife, Kelley, who makes me a better man. Her sweet words of encouragement and support provide the fuel that drives me every day, but it is her smile that gives each day more meaning.

FOREWORD

ometime during 2011, an executive recruiter called me to see if I was interested in being considered for the CEO position of the National Association of Professional Employer Organizations (NAPEO)—the national trade association for the PEO industry. By 2011 I had been in Washington, DC, for some twenty-five years, all of it spent in the labor/HR-policy space. I had served at the highest levels of the US Department of Labor in a policy role, had been appointed by President George H. W. Bush to chair a federal labor agency, and had spent ten years at the National Association of Manufacturers, lobbying on workplace issues.

Yet I had never heard of a PEO.

As the recruiter talked, I cradled the phone between my head and shoulder and frantically typed "PEO" into Google. I found NAPEO, which the search results said was "the voice of the PEO industry." That told me nothing. I went to Wikipedia but didn't get much more information there. Nonetheless, it sounded like something that might be interesting, so I agreed to toss my hat into the ring. A few months later, I was offered—and accepted—the job.

For me, arriving at NAPEO involved a bit of a learning curve. But as I learned about the PEO industry—the *more* I learned about the PEO industry—I had one nagging question: "How did I not know this industry existed?" I learned that PEOs had hundreds of thousands of small-business clients, collectively employing millions of workers. And they took all the—let's politely call it "stuff"—off employers' plates. Wages, benefits, compliance assistance—you name it: PEOs did it. This allowed the individual employers to focus on why they got into business in the first place. PEOs had, in short, the single-greatest value proposition for small- and medium-sized businesses (SMBs) that I had ever seen. But PEOs were also the best-kept secret in the SMB world. So we set about to change that.

Through years of work, we have conducted dozens of focus groups with small-business owners to see what keeps them up at night. The results included all the things you can imagine: survival, growth, turnover, revenue, and employee satisfaction. So every time we identified an area of concern to small businesses, we would work with a top workplace economist and compare PEO clients to nonclients. In every case, the empirical data showed dramatically better numbers for PEO clients than nonclients. Their businesses grew faster and had lower turnover, half the failure rate, and higher revenues, and their employees were happier and more engaged.

As a result of this research—and by arming our members with it—we saw this industry double in size between 2012 and 2017. From 2017 to 2019, we saw roughly another 75 percent growth in the industry. And why not? As local, state, and federal regulations have proliferated, small businesses increasingly have turned to PEOs, which provide compliance assistance and help them focus on the "business of their business." The Affordable Care Act (Obamacare) alone, with its torrent of rules and regulations, led to an increase in PEO business. And the COVID-19 pandemic—accompanied by the labyrinthine rules for the Paycheck Protection Program, the CARES Act, and the issues concerning returning to work or working from home—have led small businesses to turn to PEOs for help.

There are two significant tailwinds for the industry: First, the pace of regulation is unabated. To whatever extent the federal government may reduce regulation, states and localities rush to fill the gap. Second, business-school graduates in the last two decades have heard one central commandment: If it's not your core business, outsource it. So you see outsourcing of IT, travel, security … and HR. And our research proves this: the cohort most friendly to PEOs are CEOs ages twenty-five to thirty-five. These two trends will continue to power PEO growth for the foreseeable future.

So welcome to the world of PEOs. No need to apologize if you haven't heard of us. If you're reading this book, you'll learn about our industry's beginnings and growth from someone who lived it. Indeed, Lyons HR has been a long-time member of NAPEO and has helped drive the industry's growth in the southern United States. You are discovering a secret that's been well kept for far too long. You may wonder why some of your small-business peers seem to have more time on their hands to grow their company—or to golf! If you dig a little, you might find that they discovered this secret a while ago and are enjoying the benefits that a PEO brings: first and foremost, peace of mind.

This book is an informative and entertaining exposé on the PEO industry. Enjoy reading it, and then we hope you'll join the hundreds of thousands of businesses that use PEOs. When last surveyed, 98 percent of business owners said they'd recommend a PEO to another small business.

Who knows? Maybe one of them will be you.

—Pat Cleary
President and CEO
National Association of Professional Employer Organizations

INTRODUCTION

The secret to success is doing common things uncommonly well.
—John D. Rockefeller, Jr.

t's another sleepless night for Joe. As the proprietor of Joe's Auto Repair, a small automotive business with three locations and twenty-five employees, he's got a lot on his mind. OSHA just paid him another visit, and he feels certain this time they will cite him for a violation. His company's quarterly payroll taxes are late again, simply because he's been too jammed with work to figure them out and send them in. And if that isn't enough, Joe's employees are upset because their health-insurance carrier just increased their premiums by 25 percent, and he's worried he might lose some of his best technicians if he doesn't absorb the cost of the increase.

Joe's wife, Judy, is the office manager and also does the company's payroll. Tonight, she has been sitting at their kitchen table working on payroll for four hours straight, ever since the kids went to bed, and she's not even halfway finished. Two years ago, Joe convinced Judy to quit her job as a nurse to handle the administration and operations of their growing auto-repair shops. When they crunched the numbers, it seemed like she would have more time for the family, more flexibility, and more earnings by working for the company. But so far, the only thing she's had more of is headaches.

Joe had started his business armed with a great idea, a knack for machinery, and an entrepreneurial spirit, but owning his own business has been nothing like he dreamed. He has all the repair work he could ask for, a stellar reputation, skilled technicians, and opportunities to expand, but the tangled web of employment laws, regulations, and government-reporting obligations that come with having employees is threatening to put him out of business—or give him a heart attack—whichever comes first.

The sad reality of Joe's story is that he's not alone. Joe is just like the tens of thousands of other small- and medium-sized business (SMB) owners in the United States who are drowning in human-resources (HR) issues.

Joe's employment challenges will lead him to discover America's best-kept secret: Professional Employer Organizations, or PEOs, provide the single most valuable set of services to the small-business owner, allowing them to do what they do best—to serve their own clients and to sell their products or services. The administrative burdens that are thrust upon today's small-business owners are immense, and since the passage of the Civil Rights Act of 1964, there has been an exponential increase in employment-related laws and regulations, making compliance even more of a challenge. What budding entrepreneur wants to keep up with all these changes? Who wants to be distracted by shopping for employee benefit plans every year? Who wants to go through workers' compensation audits every year, to sit through unemployment hearings, to stress over a fine from the Occupational Safety and Health Administration (OSHA), to create employee handbooks, or to pay out a big penalty because something wasn't filed on time? If you're like Joe, that's not why you went into business. You went into business because you had an idea or because you wanted to be your own boss, or perhaps there was another reason. You most certainly did not start your business so that you could manage all these things … but as an employer, *you* are responsible. That's exactly why PEOs exist!

A PEO handles all these responsibilities and more for their clients, and it handles them at a cost that is usually less than what the employer would pay by doing it themselves. According to a white paper released in September of 2018 by the National Association of Professional Employer Organizations (NAPEO), only around 175,000 American SMBs are using PEOs.[1] That's just 15 percent of the marketplace! So if the value of PEO services is so great, why is market penetration so low? Perhaps, like Joe, many SMB owners have never heard of a PEO. Or maybe those who are familiar with the industry don't understand the benefits they are missing out on and are completely unaware of the following facts:[2]

- 3.7 million American workers are part of a PEO arrangement.

- PEOs provide access to healthcare for four to six million people.

- The average size of a small-business client of a NAPEO member is twenty employees.

- Small businesses that use PEOs grow faster than those that don't use PEOs. From 2010 to 2018, employment growth among PEO clients was 9 percent higher than other small businesses (based on the Intuit Small Business Employment

---

1   Laurie Bassi and Dan McMurrer, "An Economic Analysis: The PEO Industry Footprint in 2018," *NAPEO White Paper Series* no. 6 (September 2018), https://www.napeo.org/docs/default-source/white-papers/2018-white-paper-final.pdf.

2   Ibid.

Index), and 4 percent higher than employment growth in the US economy overall.

- Companies that work with a PEO have lower employee turnover and are 50 percent less likely to go out of business.

As an entrepreneur myself, I've done just about everything required to grow a successful business. Most of my experience has been trial and error, and there have been some very expensive lessons along the way. Prior to starting Lyons HR in 1995, I held positions in accounting and finance for both private and publicly held companies, and I experienced firsthand how most of the challenges confronted by organizations are somehow related to people. I learned early in my career that if you make a priority out of your people and get that part of your business right, everything else will fall into place, because good people will always find a way to solve problems. Since launching Lyons HR, I've had the opportunity to work with hundreds of employers across the United States, helping them implement smarter workforce-management strategies through payroll and tax administration, employee benefits, HR consulting, regulatory compliance, risk management, and recruiting.

From a modest eight-hundred-square-foot office in Florence, Alabama, Lyons HR has grown into a national PEO with multiple offices around the country—so if I sound passionate about the PEO industry, it's because I am!

So why am I writing this book? Well it's quite simple. I believe PEOs can have the most significant positive impact on the success of a small business. And because I am so passionate about small business, I want to spread the word and raise the public's awareness of this incredibly valuable business partnership! The comprehensive value offered by PEOs is simply unmatched, and the research proves this point, as I will demonstrate in this book. I believe PEOs are the future of small business. Just like peripheral industries such as law or finance naturally complement various unrelated businesses, I believe PEOs will someday become synonymous with HR. By providing expertise to meet their clients' toughest "people-related" challenges, PEOs make a significant impact on their bottom lines. PEOs can help drive performance, control HR and labor costs, increase profitability, and mitigate employment liabilities through a more disciplined and strategic approach to workforce management.

Whether you're already familiar with PEOs, have never heard of a PEO, or are a leader in the PEO industry, *We Are HR: The Business Owner's Definitive Guide to Professional Employer Organizations* is the new HR handbook, designed to entertain and to educate small-business owners and industry professionals on the origins and future of PEOs, while highlighting PEOs' strong value proposition and the overwhelming advantage small-business owners gain when leaving HR to the experts.

Complete with real-life examples and research-driven insight, the first half of the book will tell the history of the industry and how it evolved into what it is today. The second half will do a deep dive into the PEO value proposition and describe how the business model works, concluding with the projected future of the industry.

The book will also be peppered with personal and professional stories from my own work in the PEO industry, and I'll kick off each chapter with an update to our business owner's entrepreneurial journey.

Technology is nothing without proficiency. Ideas are worthless without creativity. It's the human element that makes or breaks a business. That's why it's crucial that businesses manage people in a way that keeps them efficient, compliant, and profitable.

The bottom line is this: when you have a tax problem, you call a CPA. If you have a legal problem, you call an attorney. And after reading this book, when you've got an HR problem, you'll call a PEO, because *We Are HR!*

CHAPTER ONE

THE CASE FOR PEOS

The best way to get started is to quit talking and start doing.
—Walt Disney

Joe scratches his head and wonders how he got into this situation. He was a successful mechanic and always had an aptitude for engines. While still in high school, Joe went to work for McAllister's Garage. Pete McAllister was a long-time friend of Joe's father and had watched Joe grow up. The budding mechanic worked diligently at his craft, honed his talents, and soon became a versatile and skilled auto technician. By the time Joe was twenty-one years old, he could completely disassemble a transmission and put it back together again. Joe completed numerous mechanical training courses and developed a reputation for being good with his hands. It seemed like he could fix just about anything.

Joe was thirty years old when he decided to strike out on his own. With more than twelve years under the hood and a growing number of loyal customers, Joe believed he had what it took to be an entrepreneur. He certainly had the work ethic. But within six months after opening Joe's Auto Repair, Joe had more work than he could handle. He was working sixteen to eighteen hours a day just to keep his head above water, and the lead time to his customers was getting longer and longer. Something had to give. That's when Joe decided he would expand his garage and hire another mechanic. Joe believed he could hire another young high school student with a knack for mechanical things and train him just like he'd been trained. He contacted the career technical director from his old high school and put the word out that he was looking to onboard someone. Soon, résumés from hopeful young students started pouring in. These were students who, like Joe had been, were eager to learn the trade and get some grease under their fingernails.

Joe hired his first employee eight months after opening his auto-repair business. Chandler was a senior in high school and, like Joe, was excited for an opportunity to prove himself. Until that moment, Joe only had to worry about himself. He was charging a fair price for his repair work, and his business had plenty of cash since he was only taking out enough money to pay *his* bills. But he hadn't put anything back for taxes, and now he had a new employee. *I know I'm supposed to withhold payroll taxes*, Joe thinks. After all, he remembered that Mr. McAllister always deducted taxes from his paycheck and gave him a Form W-2 at the end of the year.

Let's pause Joe's entrepreneurial journey right here. At this point, he has the skills, the clientele, and the reputation to scale his auto-repair shop into a successful small business and to generate a nice living for himself and his employees. But the biggest thing standing between Joe and success is in how he manages his HR-related issues in the months and years ahead. After all, Joe is a skilled mechanic and entrepreneur, but he's not a business executive. And in today's competitive corporate world, careers in HR are a specialized field, much like orthopedic surgery is a specialized field of medicine. With so many new federal laws and regulations being passed and enforced by the US Department of Labor (DOL), if Joe tries to handle things on his own, he will put himself and his business at constant risk of violating some obscure law he's never even heard of. For example, what if his new hire, Chandler, slips in a puddle of oil and breaks his wrist while on the job? Will Joe have the proper workers' compensation coverage and safety procedures in place? What if he gets sued?

Workplace injuries aside, Joe may be able to handle managing payroll and the associated withholdings for one or two or maybe even three employees; but with a busy shop to run, what will he do when he expands to five or ten employees? Or what will happen when he decides it's time to open a second shop on the other side of town to serve his growing clientele?

If Joe doesn't get a firm grasp on his HR issues quickly and effectively, his entrepreneurial dream is going to devolve into a nightmare. But Joe knows very well that he doesn't have the budget to recruit a full-time HR director or to build an HR department.

And besides, thinks Joe, *HR worries are for major companies with hundreds or thousands of employees, not just some small business with a handful of hourly workers.*

Think again, Joe.

If Joe knew about the services and benefits a PEO would offer, he could get his small business off on the right foot. He could take all the worry and woe out of HR, leaving that aspect of his budding business to the experts and freeing up his time and energy to fully focus on serving his customers. As Joe experiences the growing pains that come with running a successful small business, he will search for ways to relieve that pain. And that search will lead him to the PEO industry. Joe will have the same initial questions that most other small-business owners have when they consider using a PEO for the first time:

Would a business with only two employees benefit from a PEO, or is that too few? What if I eventually have fifty employees? Is that too many? Is hiring a PEO expensive? Will I lose control of my business? Who handles workers' compensation claims? Will I still have to worry about onboarding and interviews? Who recruits new employees? How do I make sure to comply with the DOL, OSHA, and all those other government authorities?

As we follow Joe on his small-business journey throughout this book, we're also going to unpack the story of the PEO and answer all of those questions. We'll discover how and why PEOs help clients grow faster, help them reduce employee turnover, and make them 50 percent less likely to go out of business.

But first …

WHAT EXACTLY IS A PEO?

A PEO is a for-profit enterprise that provides comprehensive human-resource services to SMBs. PEOs work with their clients to create a customized service package, which may include some or all of the following:

- Payroll and payroll tax administration

- Employee benefits, such as healthcare, other types of insurance, and retirement plans, such as a 401(k)

- Safety consultation and access to workers' compensation insurance

- HR-policy development and consultation and assistance with federal and state regulatory compliance

- Access to HR-related technology

PEOs provide services by establishing a coemployment relationship, in which both the PEO and the client have an employment relationship with the worker. The PEO assumes the responsibility and liability for the business of employment, such as risk management, human-resource management, payroll, and payroll-tax compliance, while the client business maintains day-to-day supervision of its staff and all management responsibilities.

A *small business* is defined for purposes in this book as having fewer than ninety-nine employees. When a client business contracts with a PEO, the PEO becomes the *statutory* employer of the client's employees for purposes of payroll, benefits, and workers' compensation—but the client *always* remains the common-law employer and retains complete direction and control of the worksite. The client continues to manage the employees' day-to-day activities. PEOs charge a service fee, which can be either a percentage of payroll or a flat fee per payroll processed. This service fee typically ranges from 3 to 5 percent of total gross payroll, depending on the services selected by the client.

One of the biggest benefits a small business receives from a PEO has to do with economies of scale. By working with a PEO, the client business has access to workers' compensation insurance and group health insurance at a cost that is usually lower than the client could obtain on its own. Remember, the average PEO client in the United States has twenty employees, so it only makes sense that a PEO with thousands of employees would be able to source these coverages at more competitive rates. These cost savings are passed on to the client. Companies that utilize a PEO are not forced to adopt the PEO's insurance plans, but they almost always do because of the savings made available through the relationship.

> **By working with a PEO, the client business has access to workers' compensation insurance and group health insurance at a cost that is usually lower than the client could obtain on its own.**

What a PEO is *not* is a temporary staffing company. The latter recruits and hires employees, then provides them to clients to support or supplement the clients' workforces in special work situations, such as employee absences, temporary skill shortages, or seasonal workloads. These workers are traditionally only a small portion of a business owner's workforce. PEOs also do not supply labor to worksites; they coemploy existing permanent workforces and provide services to both the business owner and the employees.

Now that we know what exactly a PEO is (and isn't), here are a few fast and fun PEO facts:[3]

- While, overall, only 27 percent of small businesses offer employee retirement plans (according to the National Federation of Independent Business, or NFIB), approximately 95 percent of NAPEO's members offer retirement plans to their small-business worksite employees, and virtually all of those offer some level of matching contribution.

---

3   Ibid.

- Actuarial data shows that PEOs aggressively manage workers' compensation risks and reduce the basic costs of workers' compensation by as much as 25 percent for small-business enterprises.

- To date, forty states have adopted some form of PEO legislation, and PEOs operate in all fifty states.

- There are 907 PEOs in the United States as of this writing.

- The total employment represented by the PEO industry is roughly the same as the combined number of employees for Walmart (United States only), Amazon, IBM, FedEx, Starbucks, AT&T, Wells Fargo, Apple, and Google.

- Between 2008 and 2017, the number of workers coemployed by a PEO grew at a compounded annual rate of 8.3 percent. This is roughly fourteen times higher than the compounded annual-growth rate of employment in the economy overall during the same period.

- Privately held businesses that use PEOs are approximately 50 percent less likely to fail (to permanently cease operations) from one year to the next when compared to similar companies in the overall US population of private businesses.

The PEO industry is currently experiencing a surge of rapid growth as more and more SMBs learn about the benefits of engaging a PEO, especially with the increased (and confusing) labor regulation and compliance costs (e.g., healthcare requirements).

Considering both the broader services available and the cost savings realized from small businesses outsourcing their HR responsibilities, Peter Cappelli of the Wharton School at the University of Pennsylvania recently stated, "This is one of those rare instances that is both cheaper and better. It's a big burden on a local HR manager to know everything."

A similar point is made by Martin VanMeter of VanMeter Realty, a small realty company based in Durant, Oklahoma: "Working with a PEO has provided us an economical way of employing people without the stress of paperwork and payroll. Our PEO is always available to answer questions or provide support to the employees."

THE LIFEBLOOD OF SMALL BUSINESSES

No book about PEOs would be complete without including NAPEO, which I will refer to humbly and often throughout this narrative for its industry research and unparalleled expertise in the PEO space.

Its comprehensive series of white papers has been an invaluable tool in making the case for PEOs, and there is no better advocate in any industry. In a 2013 NAPEO white paper on fueling small-business growth, authors and researchers Laurie Bassi and Dan McMurrer of McBassi & Company state the following:

> As traditional sources of competitive advantage have eroded in the face of globalization and technology change, the importance of a company's people has steadily increased. People—including their skills, knowledge, and creativity—represent a critical asset on which a company must depend for success in today's competitive marketplace.[4]

---

4   Laurie Bassi and Dan McMurrer, "Professional Employer Organizations: Fueling Small Business Growth," *NAPEO White Paper Series* no. 1 (September 2013), https://www.napeo.org/docs/default-source/white-papers/whitepaper1.pdf.

Put simply, a business's success comes down to its people. If client business owners are the heart of business, employees are its lifeblood. In an article about HR by Theresa Welbourne, she says the research suggests that "the strongest predictor of a company's probability of surviving for at least five years after its initial public offering is its level of investment in human resources."[5]

HR is not something to be considered *after* a small business begins to grow. It is a critical step that demands full attention, just like accounting or legal services. Yet too many times, small-business owners attempt to handle HR matters themselves and end up in hot water—or worse, out of business. You don't want to find yourself in the position of our auto-shop owner, Joe, midstream in his entrepreneurial journey, with twenty-five employees, three locations, the threat of OSHA violations, recurringly late quarterly tax payments, rising healthcare costs, and an overall lack of HR infrastructure that could put him out of compliance with numerous federal and state laws.

These issues and much more are what the PEO industry seeks to address, creating a recipe for success and peace of mind for the small-business owner—a win-win for everyone involved. Quite noble and righteous, right?

Yet the origin story of the PEO industry is a little more colorful … and a lot less noble.

---

5   Theresa Welbourne, "Want to Make Money on IPOs? Learn About Companies' HR Management Strategies," *Workforce. com*, September 2, 2010, https://www.workforce.com/news/ want-to-make-money-on-ipos-learn-about-companies-hr-management-strategies.

CHAPTER TWO

THE EARLY DAYS

If everything seems under control, you're not going fast enough.

—Mario Andretti

Joe's Auto Repair finished its first full year in business with almost a half million dollars in sales. *Not bad*, Joe thought to himself as his new certified public accountant, Martin, shared the results with him. And next year with the help of his wife, Judy, and his young protégé, Chandler, was expected to be even better. Chandler was showing a lot of potential, and Joe was feeling more confident in the quality of his work. Chandler was grinding his way through ASE certifications and was expected to complete the program in a couple more months. Joe was pleased with his progress and hoped to hire at least two more technicians like Chandler to help keep the momentum going. Yes, business was good!

Judy was not an accountant, but she was learning quickly. She had installed QuickBooks on their computer at the shop and had taught herself how to use most of the features of the popular bookkeeping program. With no formal training, she became the company's bookkeeper and found herself really enjoying what she was doing. She created a simple chart of accounts and, for the most part, had captured all their sales and operating expenses for Martin, the CPA, to use to prepare their tax return.

"You've done a nice job keeping the books, Judy," Martin said. "Now all I need are your payroll records."

"Everything is there," Judy replied.

Martin stared back earnestly. "You mean you didn't make any quarterly estimated tax payments? Or withhold any taxes from your employee's paycheck?"

"No," admitted Judy, clearly confused. "We just took money out of the company's checking account when we needed to pay our bills. We only have one other employee, and we pay him out of the same account. It's all right there."

Martin had a puzzled look on his face. "You do realize that, as an employer, you are required to withhold federal income taxes and payroll taxes from your employee's pay and remit it to the government monthly? You then are required to report all wages paid and taxes remitted every quarter on Form 941."

"Yes, I realize that," said Judy. "I knew we were supposed to remit taxes, but I wasn't sure when they were due. That's why we're coming to you. Can you take care of this and just let us know how much we owe?"

"Sure, I can take care of it," assured Martin, "but don't be surprised if there's a big penalty due along with your tax bill. I suggest you let our firm do your payroll or find an independent payroll company to handle it for you moving forward."

Joe and Judy just learned a valuable lesson. They thought that because the business was run under a sole proprietorship, they didn't have to withhold Social Security and Medicare taxes, much less match them. But the reality is, *they do*. That's right—employers, even small ones like Joe's Auto Repair, are the government's volunteer tax collectors. And if you are a small-business owner like Joe and don't collect those taxes the way the government requires or remit them exactly as it demands, you are rewarded by being forced to pay a stiff penalty. When you are dealing with the IRS, not knowing the rules does not excuse lack of compliance. Don't you just love the IRS? PEO clients, on the other hand, don't have to worry about this dilemma, especially if they use a PEO that is certified by the IRS. But that's a topic we will address later.

So it should come as little shock that small-business owners like Joe, who were desperate for help and guidance, were both relieved and excited at the thought of handing off all HR-related responsibilities to another company when the earliest incarnation of a burgeoning PEO industry was taking root in the late 1970s and early 1980s. Yet like all new frontiers, there are always going to be

> Yet like all new frontiers, there are always going to be pioneers looking to expand a dream for the betterment of all ... and there are always going to be outlaws looking to take advantage of the vulnerable for personal gain.

25

pioneers looking to expand a dream for the betterment of all … and there are always going to be outlaws looking to take advantage of the vulnerable for personal gain. So it should also come as little shock that in those early days of the PEO industry, which at the time was known more familiarly as "Employee Leasing," the outlaws came on fast and hard, finding loopholes to exploit and stacking the deck for their own gain.

ORIGINS OF THE INDUSTRY—FINDING A LOOPHOLE

To understand the genesis of the employee-leasing model, we first need to revisit the history of the Social Security tax in America. The Social Security Administration was established in 1935 following the Great Depression, in an effort to offer the American worker a way to save for retirement. Essentially, each year, US workers contribute a specified amount through payroll deductions to their individual Social Security account, and this amount is matched by their employers. But since its inception, there have been growing concerns about the sustainability of the program. Social Security has evolved into a third rail of government spending and is a frequently addressed topic in stump speeches every election cycle.

Social Security was never intended to provide all the benefits needed in retirement, only to supplement the private savings of the retiree. Throughout history, Congress has used the tax code to encourage private savings through pensions, profit sharing, and other private and corporate-sponsored retirement plans. These plans are referred to as qualified plans because they "qualify" for tax-preferred treatment. But from the very beginning, it was never the intention of Congress to allow these plans to discriminate in favor of the more highly compensated—usually owners, shareholders, and officers of an organization. Congress's intent was nondiscriminatory plans, but that is not what always happened. In those early days, with careful planning and the use of different types of plan designs, the contributions could be substantially tilted in favor of certain employees.

Then in 1974 Congress passed the Employee Retirement Income Security Act (ERISA) to address what was perceived to be abuses in the pension system. In addition to ensuring the financial soundness of these plans, another major goal of this legislation was to protect lower- to middle-income workers from being unfairly disadvantaged by their employer's pension plan. Yet ERISA contained no provision requiring separate organizations with common ownership to be aggregated when determining if IRS antidiscrimination rules were being violated. It was this omission that provided the loophole needed to avoid violating antidiscrimination rules.

To perpetuate the discriminatory pension practices, some employers would establish multiple business entities, all owned by the same person or persons, and have different plans and contribution standards for each entity. This allowed the owner to employ preferred employees in an entity in which higher contributions would be funded without worrying about discriminating against other employees. After all, those employees were employed by different companies.

Other examples of this strategy were not so blatant. In some cases, large physician groups would establish an affiliated service organization with a separate federal ID number. They would then consolidate all their employee-support services into that separate service organization that served the overall group. This obviously created more efficiency through consolidation and greater buying power for benefit plans. With multiple legal entities all managed by a single employee-management company, they were able to create plan designs that were ideally suited for physicians with similar life circumstances. Older physicians nearing retirement age could maximize their pension contributions, while younger physicians might still be paying off medical school debt and would likely want to make lower contributions, if any. This arrangement allowed those with similar life circumstances to band together into one corporation with a plan that better suited their needs. This concept would later be known as employee leasing, the early incarnation of PEOs.

THE RISE OF EMPLOYEE LEASING

With employee leasing, which diverted into the tax shelters of the wealthy the funds that would otherwise have gone to the retirement plans of their employees, a whole new frontier was born—and it was catching on like wildfire.

As stated earlier, any new frontier with loose structure and little regulation will draw both pioneers and outlaws. Affiliated service organizations sprang up everywhere, as creative business owners sought out ways to circumvent the law. It was not until December of 1980 that President Carter signed into law section 414(m) of the Internal Revenue Code, which required affiliated companies under common ownership to be treated as if they were employed by a single employer. As a result of this legislation, employers would no longer be able to separate affiliated employees into different entities in order to create discriminatory benefit plans for themselves and their more highly compensated employees.

After the passage of section 414(m), there was a surge in newly formed and independently owned employee-leasing companies. Although similar in concept, employee-leasing companies differed from administrative service organizations (ASOs) in that there was no shared ownership. An employee-leasing company was entirely independent—free to provide services to any organization and not just to a captive controlled group. And although there was no formal legislation addressing the business of employee leasing, the Internal Revenue Code did not prohibit the practice.

Now, to better understand how the PEO industry evolved, let's dive a little deeper into what the climate was like in this new frontier.

LAX UNDERWRITING STANDARDS

Traditionally, insurance carriers (primarily workers' compensation carriers) insure small businesses based strictly on their risk profile. An HVAC contractor, for example, gives her claims history to a workers' compensation carrier, who evaluates the history and rates the business according to its SIC code and claims history to determine the details of the policy. In the early days of employee leasing, however, the workers' compensation insurance carriers didn't really know how to handle this business model, because the industry was so new and because an employee-leasing company's clientele can be so diverse in risk.

For instance, let's assume XYZ Employee-Leasing Company had ten clients. One of them could be a doctor's office. Another one may be an auto-repair shop. Yet another might be a landscaping company or an HVAC company. That diversity of risk within the structure of the employee-leasing company created challenges for the carriers, which in turn made it difficult for the leasing company to get coverage. In addition, because the early employee-leasing companies were enrolling small businesses across multiple industries, it was easier for dishonest operators to misclassify a company's payroll to their workers' compensation carrier. The payroll of a landscaping firm, for example, could be reported to the carrier under the classification code of an insurance office. Clearly, landscaping is a more hazardous activity than working in an insurance office. A dishonest operator might be tempted to do this to take advantage of a lower rate, but when this type of misclassification of payroll is reported on a large scale, the carrier's claims will outpace its premium quickly, and it will eventually blow up.

So during the early days of the PEO industry, when it was still known as employee leasing, there was a lot of uncertainty about exactly what the insurance company was insuring. Yet because insurance occurs in cycles as carriers have good years and bad years, their appetite for risk often changes.

After a particularly bad hurricane season, for example, there might be a hardening of the market. But if things have been stable for three or four good years, insurance companies become more competitive, and then they start lowering their rates to write more business.

So it was during those times when the market was soft that employee-leasing companies were able to enroll all their different companies, with very little risk-management oversight.

This led to a questionable method of drumming up business, called "farming" by some employee-leasing companies—that is, recruiting new clients with high-risk businesses and/or poor claims histories by offering to save them money through using the employee-leasing company's catch-all insurance policy at a significantly lower rate than what the client was currently paying. What small business struggling with high risk and a terrible claims history wouldn't want to sign right up? This tactic was a major driver in the early days for growth in acceleration in the pre-PEO space. But as the saying goes, what goes up must come down, and anytime there are low rates and adverse selection, it's eventually going to blow up. And that's exactly what happened.

Soft markets and lax underwriting standards due to the inability of carriers to properly assess the risks led to the enrollment of all colors of high-risk accounts. Before long came a rash of expensive claims, followed by huge losses for the insurance companies, eventually ending in the mass cancellation of policies.

And while these practices were certainly questionable, there were other practices that caught the attention of state and federal regulators.

ACCOUNTING FOR TRUST FUNDS

PEOs have large sums of money that pass through their accounts. At Lyons HR, we have hundreds of millions of dollars that pass through our company each year, and we know very well that's not *our* money. Rather, that money is held in trust-fund accounts for our clients and employees, to be used for payroll and all related payroll expenses. That money is not part of our budget or financial picture. But because we collect these funds from our clients and employees, we effectively hold these funds in trust until they are remitted to the appropriate taxing authority. We're required by law to remit these funds to the proper authorities, and if we don't, then I can go to prison. And there's not enough money in the world to make me want to do that. That said, accurate accounting of funds that are temporarily held in trust on behalf of employees is critical in the PEO space.

But in the pre-PEO early days of employee leasing, for some companies or some proprietors with questionable ethics, seeing large sums of money passing through their control was a temptation too great. Really, there were two scenarios going on at that point.

The first involves outright theft. A small business of ten employees can easily have $750,000 to $1 million in payroll, which translates to about $80,000 worth of payroll taxes. So just imagine all of these small companies, perhaps twenty or thirty of them, and consider how much money is flowing through one of those early employee-leasing companies. They are completely responsible not only for handling the payroll and getting the people paid on time but also for remitting the proper taxes to the state and federal government. Of course, let's not forget this was long before ACH and wires and other conveniences we've become accustomed to.

Because it was all manually done, there were no electronic records, so there was also far less oversight. And it's not too far of a leap to imagine that an owner or accountant—one with a lack of integrity and $300,000–$400,000 sitting in an account earmarked for payroll taxes—may be tempted to line their own pockets or to misappropriate those funds.

The second all-too-common scenario was pure incompetence. Let's say somebody who was in the insurance business lost some of their clientele because an employee-leasing company swooped into town and stole them by switching them over to a new carrier.

"Well, I'm going to start my own employee-leasing company!" they might say. This person has no financial acumen, no systems in place, no experience whatsoever, but they go back to their clients and say, "Hey, I started an employee-leasing company, too. Come back to me, and I can give you all the things that company is giving you."

It wouldn't take long for that new employee-leasing company to build up twenty-five, thirty, maybe even fifty small clients with $3–$4 million worth of payroll going through it, which means nearly $500,000 worth of payroll tax. Of course, those payroll taxes are supposed to be remitted to the government, but in some cases, if the owner didn't have proper accounting processes in place, they might fail to properly remit. The next thing you know, they would fall behind on the taxes, or they might use trust-fund tax monies for operating expenses or other purposes. Too often, this practice would spiral out of control until eventually the employee-leasing company would run out of money and be forced to go out of business.

These two nightmare scenarios yielded the same outcome for the client. Even though the client had remitted all their payroll taxes to the employee-leasing company, the IRS would still track down the client and demand payment for the unpaid taxes, plus penalties and interest. In those early days and before passage of the Small Business Efficiency Act (SBEA) in 2014, the client—not the employee-leasing company—would still be responsible for unremitted payroll taxes, even though the client could prove they had been billed for and had paid the taxes. As you can probably guess, the IRS wouldn't care that the client had paid the taxes through the employee-leasing company; the IRS would force that client to pay those taxes again!

GAMING THE SYSTEM

Another key employer tax that was ripe for abuse was unemployment taxes. As you may know, each state establishes its own unemployment-insurance program subject to guidelines established by the Federal Unemployment Tax Act (FUTA). Each state determines its own tax-rate structure and the wage base needed to fund its program. Each state has a starting rate and a range of what the rate could be. For example, in the state of Alabama, the wage base or "threshold" is $8,000, and the initial rate for a new company starting out is 2.7 percent. That means for every employee an Alabama employer has, they're going to pay 2.7 percent on the first $8,000 of wages, or $216 per year in State Unemployment Tax Act (SUTA) taxes. A rate adjustment occurs eighteen months after a company begins and is adjusted each year thereafter, based on the company's claims experience. If the company hasn't laid anybody off and there have been no claims against the company, then the rate will go down. But if there have been multiple layoffs or claims, the rate increases.

So let's say a company has been in business for ten years, and it has had ebbs and flows in business—it loses a major account and has to lay off people, then lands an even bigger account and needs to hire people back. Over the course of several years, it goes through this cycle of hiring people, laying them off, hiring people, and laying them off. In the meantime, the state is promulgating a rate based upon the company's actual unemployment-claims activity. So if a company tends to lay people off regularly because its business is cyclical or seasonal, instead of having a 2.7 percent rate, it may have a 4.5 percent rate. Essentially, the state considers it a "repeat offender." These kinds of spikes in SUTA rates aren't all that uncommon and happen a lot with businesses that have any kind of seasonality component or that are sensitive to economic swings.

By contrast, a company that's had a very stable work history—and perhaps has even had the same twenty employees for the last ten years—might go from a 2.7 percent rate to a 0.5 percent rate.

So now that you understand what SUTA rates are and how they are determined, let's talk about their place in the PEO story.

SUTA DUMPING

Let's go back in time to the days before SUTA dumping was illegal. A company may have been impacted by an economic downturn, have struggled with leadership or finances (or both), or may have been forced to lay off lots of employees. The resulting increase in its SUTA rate could threaten the company's very survival. For many small businesses, going from paying maybe $25,000 a year in state-unemployment taxes to $75,000 a year can be the difference between lasting another year or shutting down for good, but not if you can get a do-over.

With a strategy that came to be known as SUTA dumping, a company could close down Company A and start over with Company B. The new entity would be assigned the new entity SUTA rate of 2.7 percent, and presto, problem solved! The company has effectively "dumped" its old SUTA rate. Of course, if it continues the same business practices, then the same result will ultimately occur, but it'll get the benefit of that lower rate for a period of time until the claims catch up to it. And when the SUTA rate spikes again, it can just rinse and repeat.

Anti-SUTA dumping laws have since ensured that the rate follows the ownership, but during the early days of employee leasing, companies would entice struggling businesses to come aboard as clients for the low SUTA rate, as each client's employees would not technically be working for that client any longer.

SUTA HARVESTING

SUTA harvesting was another tactic employed to beat a high SUTA rate for companies that had a lot of employee turnover. It worked like this: a start-up organization would set up Company A and Company B. Then it would put all of the high-turnover business in Company A and all of its stable employees, including the owner and other high-priority employees, like family and friends, in Company

B. Both companies are going to start with a 2.7 percent SUTA rate. After two or three years with the stable people in Company B, that rate goes from 2.7 percent down to 0.5 percent or even 0.2 percent. Once that entity has a rate that's well below the starting point of 2.7 percent, then the owner would take all the employees from Company A and move them over to Company B. The owner just harvested an artificial rate and beat the system. Unfortunately, some employee-leasing companies engaged in this practice as a way to gain a competitive advantage and to significantly lower the SUTA cost of their clients.

Although SUTA dumping and SUTA harvesting were tax strategies utilized for many years across virtually every industry, the practice had many opponents who believed it was a dishonest attempt to disguise a company's true unemployment experience, thereby cheating the system. In 2004, President George W. Bush signed the SUTA Dumping Prevention Act, which not only prohibited the practice but also provided civil and criminal penalties for violators. The federal law also required each state to follow suit and pass its own anti-SUTA dumping legislation as a condition for maintaining its federal tax credits under FUTA. Even with the passage of this legislation, the law still did not prohibit a company from experiencing a lower SUTA rate as a result of entering into a PEO relationship. Although some states still require wages to be reported under the client's SUTA account number, most states allow the PEO to report the wages of all its clients in that state under the PEO's SUTA account number. As a result, PEOs must do an effective job of managing their unemployment claims to keep SUTA rates as low as possible.

CHAPTER THREE

RESTORING ORDER

Mistakes are the growing pains of wisdom.

—William George Jordan

Joe felt like celebrating! He'd always heard that most businesses fail within the first five years, so when he completed his fifth year in business, he thought, *I must be doing something right.*

Yes, Joe had built a solid reputation for doing quality work at a fair price. And best of all, his business was profitable. Judy had become more proficient at managing the office, preparing weekly payroll, and keeping the books. She had basically taught herself how to use Quick-Books, with some occasional guidance from their CPA, Martin.

Joe was also ready to expand. His shop already had three functional service bays, but with five fully trained mechanics working for him, adding two more bays made a lot of sense. Joe bought the vacant lot next door and scheduled a meeting with his general contractor to go over his expansion plans.

As Joe reflected on his first five years in business, he couldn't help but think back to those first couple of years when it was just him working on cars for twelve to fifteen hours per day, and he marveled at how different his workday was now. Joe was still working just as many hours, but rarely did he have time to step into the shop and actually get under the hood. Joe's first love was doing the repair work, and he really missed it; but with seven employees, there always seemed to be something else demanding his time. He was constantly juggling employee schedules to make sure the shop work was covered. When he wasn't managing employee absenteeism, tardiness, and turnover, there were always parts to be ordered, equipment to be maintained, and most of all, customers to keep happy.

THE NEED FOR LEGAL CERTAINTY

By the late 1980s, it was clear that the PEO industry was here to stay. What started as a tax-savings strategy to help employers maximize pension contributions had evolved into a multifaceted business-service model that clients grew to depend upon. Tax-sheltered pension planning gave birth to the industry. Low-cost health and workers' compensation insurance were responsible for its early growth. But the PEO industry's staying power can be attributed to the ever-increasing burdens and responsibilities placed on employers by state and federal regulations. In fact, the PEO business model has created its share of challenges for legislators over the years.

If you consider all the major employment laws that have been passed over the last century, they all have one thing in common:

they start with the assumption that there is a one-to-one relationship between the employer and the employee. That is, the idea of having more than one employer introduces a degree of complexity that has proved difficult to address in legislation. Among the numerous employment laws that have been passed over the years, arguably the most consequential have been the Fair Labor Standards Act of 1938 (FLSA); Title VII of the Civil Rights Act of 1964, which established the Equal Employment Opportunity Commission (EEOC); the Employee Retirement Income Security Act of 1974 (ERISA); and the Affordable Care Act of 2010 (ACA). (*See section I of the appendix for a summary of important labor laws.*)

Each of these laws established important employment standards that continue to dictate employment practices. But as sweeping as these laws have been, none of them addressed alternative-employment arrangements, as is the case when a company works with a PEO. Let's take ERISA for example. The primary purpose of ERISA is to safeguard the interests of plan participants in employer-sponsored benefit and retirement plans. The law does not require employers to offer employee benefit plans, but it sets important standards for those that do. And there can be stiff penalties for employers who do not comply.

Since the law passed in 1974, retirement-plan administration has become so complex that many business owners have found it easier to outsource it. In addition, the Department of Labor is constantly passing new regulations forcing plan administrators to comply with the changes. Still, ERISA—with all its complexity, amendments, and regulations—does not refer to employee leasing, PEOs, or any other form of alternative-employer arrangement. It was during the years immediately following passage of ERISA that a new cottage industry of pension-plan experts emerged.

Suddenly there was a surge in ERISA attorneys and CPAs special-izing in pensions to help plan administrators navigate all the rules. And there were still those who questioned whether leased employees were even eligible to participate in the leasing company's retirement plan. Yet the industry forged ahead, doing its best to apply ERISA to its business model, despite ERISA's lack of regulations specific to the industry.

ERISA also introduced the concept of multiple-employer welfare arrangements (MEWAs). With healthcare costs rising, there was a groundswell of support from associations and other common-interest groups to be allowed to legally band together to negotiate lower health-insurance premiums than they could obtain individu-ally. The idea behind MEWAs made sense—that is, capitalizing on economies of scale. But what resulted was the establishment of mul-tiple-employer trusts (METs). These trusts were often self-funded and in many cases were able to avoid going through an insurance company altogether. MEWAs allowed small companies greater price and plan-design flexibility, and because they were under the jurisdic-tion of a federal law, they were able to avoid many state regulations.

With the line of regulatory oversight somewhat blurred, you can probably guess what happened next. Many MEWAs and METs were underfunded and/or lacked the necessary reserves to pay all their par-ticipant's claims and were eventually dissolved. As you can imagine, MEWAs quickly developed a bad reputation in the marketplace. But the abusive MEWAs and METs were not considered employee benefit plans as defined by ERISA because they were not established by an employer. Most were started by opportunistic entrepreneurs who marketed deeply discounted medical coverage to desperate employers, with whom the MET sponsor had no prior relationship. Although ERISA maintained jurisdiction over MEWAs through its broad pre-emption provision, it also contained a clause stating that nothing in

ERISA shall be construed to exempt or to relieve any person from any law of any state that regulates insurance. In other words, ERISA reserves the right to exercise preemption over state law, but rarely, if ever, is it enforced. In response to the abuses created by METs, Congress enacted legislation in 1983 that amended ERISA, making it impossible for METs to make the claim that because ERISA preempts state insurance laws, METs and MEWAs could escape state regulation.

A WATERSHED MOMENT

It was not until 1982, with the passage of the Tax Equity and Fiscal Responsibility Act (TEFRA), that the PEO industry received its first mention in any federal legislation, although in those days it was still referred to as employee leasing, and the legislation addressed the practice of employee leasing rather than the industry itself. The primary purpose of TEFRA was to address the growing federal deficit through a series of spending cuts and tax increases, but it also contained language prohibiting discrimination in corporate pension plans, referred to as its *safe-harbor provision.*

This provision stated that leased employees were to be considered as employees of the client company for the purpose of antidiscrimination testing. Since TEFRA (1982) and until SBEA (2014), the federal statutes have not addressed the PEO industry specifically. That's why PEOs have been largely regulated at the state level, either by the state's department of labor or department of insurance. From a federal perspective, the PEO industry has had to operate within a federal legislative framework that did not even consider its existence when most of the laws were passed.

The industry celebrated TEFRA because finally the concept of employee leasing was acknowledged in federal legislation. No longer could opponents claim employee leasing was not legal. And over the next four years, the number of employee-leasing firms in the United States grew from fewer than fifty to *more than four hundred*. In fact, the IRS wrote several favorable letters of determination in those early days. But with no established legal precedent, there were still those who opposed the idea of employee leasing and lobbied Congress to pass antileasing legislation.

The Tax Reform Act (TRA) of 1986 lowered the top marginal tax rate from 50 percent to 28 percent, but it also ushered in a wave of restrictions on employee-leasing pension plans. The most devastating provision was one that capped participation in employee-leasing pension plans to 20 percent of the client's total workforce. This provision was not included in the version of the bill that passed the House or the Senate, and how it became part of the final legislation remains a mystery to this day. It's widely speculated within the industry that this provision was added after committee debate was concluded and that legislators opposed to the concept had intended it to slow the growth of employee leasing. The impact from TRA was immediate and severe, resulting in a mass exodus from employee-leasing firms. Most of the employee-leasing firms that had built their companies exclusively around the safe-harbor pension benefits simply went out of business.

But there were many clients who joined employee-leasing firms for the pension benefits yet remained in the relationship even after the pension benefit was gone. Why? Because those employee-leasing companies that had diversified and offered services like payroll, health benefits, risk management, and HR compliance had developed a comprehensive and irreplaceable service model on which their clients depended. They are the ones that survived, and their clients had come to value the convenience of all those other services. Thus, the PEO concept as we recognize it today was born.

REBRANDING AN INDUSTRY

Once the industry abandoned the safe-harbor pension play, it created much greater marketing opportunities, which allowed the industry to better chart its course for the future. The Tax Reform Act of 1986 may have dealt a death blow to PEOs that focused solely on pension planning, but it also gave the industry the opportunity to reset and to define itself in a more comprehensive and value-added way. With federal recognition in TEFRA and a newfound purpose, it was time for the industry to be formally recognized and to do everything it could to address the abuses of the past.

In the fall of 1984, the National Staff Leasing Association (NSLA) was established with just fourteen charter members. In 1994 this organization would be renamed the National Association of Professional Employer Organizations (NAPEO). This renaming was in response to the industry at long last abandoning the term "employee leasing," for a number of reasons. For one, the whole notion of employee leasing had been distasteful from the beginning. After all, since the passage of the Thirteenth Amendment, "leasing" individuals has not been legal in this country, let alone morally sound. Second, all those rule breakers and loophole abusers from the frontier days had operated under the employee-leasing banner, so rebranding allowed the industry to distance itself from the sins of the past.

Today, NAPEO remains the premier industry trade association, advocating tirelessly on behalf of the PEO industry at both state and federal levels. Since its inception, NAPEO has sought to support its members and to educate the public about the advantages small businesses gain by utilizing a PEO. NAPEO has established fiscal and operational best-practice standards for the industry and has been largely responsible for the licensing and registration guidelines that exist at the state level. NAPEO crafted the PEO Model Act, which has been adopted, either in whole or in part, by thirty-eight states as of this writing. (*A complete listing of states and their licensing requirements is included in section III of the appendix.*)

In addition, as a part of the industry's commitment to self-regulation, the Employer Services Assurance Corporation (ESAC) was established in 1995. ESAC is an independent accreditation service that independently verifies a participating PEO's compliance with all employer fiduciary and contractual responsibilities. PEOs that seek to be accredited by ESAC must undergo a rigorous operational and financial review, which includes background checks on controlling persons. And as a condition to maintaining ESAC accreditation, PEOs must report on a quarterly basis the results of an extensive list of fiduciary tests conducted by an independent CPA. The financial performance of an accredited PEO is backed by $15 million in surety bonds, which protect the PEO's clients from a potential default. The ESAC assurance program has been successful. Since its inception, there has never been a default by an accredited PEO.

It's true that the PEO industry traces its origins back to days when savvy business owners sought creative ways to circumvent tax laws and to maximize their personal pensions. But it is also true that the industry could not have survived if it had remained a pension-only play. No business model can survive if its very existence is dependent upon the continually changing winds of legislative uncertainty.

The industry had to diversify its service offerings in a way that would make it sustainable—regardless of what happens in Washington, DC.

PEO INDUSTRY SPOTLIGHT

BRITT LANDRUM, JR.

The PEO industry owes a debt of gratitude to some of the early pioneers who stood for integrity and helped shape the industry into what it is today. One of those early pioneers was Britt Landrum, Jr. Mr. Landrum was working as a vocational rehabilitation counselor in 1970 when, at age thirty-two, he decided to start Landrum Personnel Associates, an employee-recruiting business based in his hometown of Pensacola, Florida. The company enjoyed early success, but Landrum was in search of a business model that provided a more-recurring source of revenue. That search led him to establish Landrum Staffing Services in 1973, which began providing temporary workers to businesses in the greater Pensacola area. Over the ensuing years, the Landrum name became synonymous with employment services throughout the panhandle of Florida.

In 1981, Landrum read an article in *Inc.* magazine about an employee-leasing business in California called Contract Staffing of America. Intrigued by the concept, Landrum recognized the potential of this burgeoning business and immediately began exploring ways to leverage his already-successful staffing business by adding employee leasing to his service offerings. After two years of planning, Landrum launched AmStaff Human Resources in December of 1983, as one of the first employee-leasing firms in north Florida.

"There were only about forty or fifty employee-leasing companies in the entire country at that time, and there was practically no regulatory oversight. We were all searching for some sort of guidance," Landrum recalled. "It was difficult to get health insurance for leased workers, and it was practically impossible to get workers' compensation coverage outside of the state-assigned risk pool or self-insurance fund."

Landrum attributes the early success of his PEO to the reputation he had built over the preceding ten years in the staffing business. As the industry grew in the state of Florida, Landrum became a key voice at the statehouse, advocating on behalf of the industry. Always committed to honesty and ethical business practices, Landrum was troubled by the practice of some operators who sponsored underfunded health and workers' compensation plans, which left clients exposed and uncovered. Following the publicity generated by some high-profile defaults, Landrum became a leading voice in getting the first licensing law passed in the state of Florida in 1991. Landrum continued his commitment to the development of the industry by becoming a charter member of the National Staff Leasing Association, the Florida Association of Professional Employer Organizations, and in 1995 he was instrumental in the establishment of the Employer Services Assurance Corporation (ESAC).

Over the past fifty years, LandrumHR has grown into a national PEO with worksite employees in forty-nine states. It continues to run its operations from its corporate headquarters in Pensacola, Florida. In 2017 Landrum retired from day-to-day responsibilities, and his son, Britt Landrum III, replaced his father as president and CEO.

Landrum feels a great deal of satisfaction when he looks back over his almost forty years in the PEO industry.

"We were able to provide good opportunities for our staff members and much-needed HR services for our clients," he said. "I believe PEO and HR outsourcing as a business strategy are here to stay and will always be people-centered where developing and maintaining personal relationships are of key importance. Those relationships can only be supplemented by the amazing technology we have available to us today."

CHAPTER FOUR

PILLARS OF PROFITABILITY

If people like you, they'll listen to you. But if they
trust you, they'll do business with you.

—Zig Ziglar

Joe's Auto Repair is a success, but Joe feels like he's working himself to death. With no formal education in business, Joe had grown from running a one-man operation to now employing fifteen full-time mechanics. But Joe knows if he is going to keep the momentum going, he has to keep his employees happy, and that means providing them with an affordable benefits plan. Since opening his shop ten years earlier, Joe had hired and trained over thirty mechanics, but it seemed about the time he got them trained and productive, they would leave him for more money or a better opportunity. Each time, Joe would increase the hourly wage he was paying to be as fair as possible, but benefits plans intimidated Joe, and he just didn't know enough about them to make a good decision. In fact, the lack of an employee benefit plan was an ongoing source of stress for Joe because he knew his employees all had young families. He had shopped over the years for competitive plans, but the premiums were always too expensive. And the more questions he asked, the more confused he became.

What is a fiduciary? What does safe harbor mean? Who is a plan sponsor and what is my liability as the employer for vesting and matching contributions in a 401(k) plan? What is a cafeteria plan, and what is a Form 5500?

Joe had many questions, and his search for answers would eventually lead him to a PEO.

Some weeks later, Joe was having lunch with an old friend from high school. Like Joe, Dan was an entrepreneur, and he had struck out on his own seven years earlier. He had opened his own HVAC contracting business after working for a successful general contractor and learning the trade. As the two men talked about their businesses, it was uncanny how similar their experiences had been, particularly when it came to hiring and retaining qualified employees.

Like Joe, Dan had experienced turnover of some of his best trained technicians.

"It was so frustrating," Dan complained. "As soon as I got a technician trained and productive, I'd lose him to a bigger company that could offer higher pay and better benefits."

Dan then explained how he had solved his turnover problem, which had been threatening his business. Two years earlier, Dan decided to partner with a PEO. He described how his PEO had lowered his overall employment costs and taken the headaches of employment off him. Dan's employees were happy with the affordable benefit options offered through the PEO, and Dan was happy with the lower workers' compensation insurance cost available through the PEO. Most of all, Dan enjoyed the peace of mind that came with knowing his employment responsibilities were being managed by HR professionals.

As Joe left the restaurant, he thanked Dan for the tip and was eager to do his own research into PEOs. If something sounds too good to be true, it usually is. *I mean, there are no shortcuts to success,* Joe thought to himself. *Is this PEO thing legal? Why have I never heard of this? Is there a catch?* Joe had a lot of questions, and his quest for answers would eventually lead him to one of the best business decisions he ever made.

If you are unfamiliar with PEOs, you may have many of the very same questions Joe had. This chapter is pivotal in providing the answers to those questions, as well as many, many more. From this point on, we move away from a historical perspective of the industry and into its modern incarnation and applications—dissecting the nuts and bolts of what PEOs are all about and how they are designed to help small businesses succeed.

PEOs help their clients make more money, keep more of the money they make, and protect their assets in the process. That's a bold claim, but the statistics prove it to be true. When you think about what goes into making a company profitable, it's virtually impossible to remove the human element. That's right; a company's profitability depends on its people, and that encompasses a wide range of issues. From helping client businesses attract and retain the best and the brightest to making employees more productive, PEOs provide value to their clients. PEOs turn HR into a strategic initiative that not only improves profitability but also protects the assets that generate that profitability. That value is delivered through a wide range of services that can all be linked to one of four categories: (1) payroll and payroll-tax administration, (2) employee benefits, (3) safety and risk management, and (4) HR compliance. I like to refer to these as the *Pillars of Profitability*. When a small business has all four of these pillars supporting it, it can focus its attention on profit-generating activities, like taking care of customers and growing the business.

Now let's more closely examine each one of the pillars.

PILLAR I: PAYROLL AND PAYROLL-TAX ADMINISTRATION

When Joe opened his auto-repair shop and hired his first employee, he—like millions of other small-business owners—became an indispensable member of the government's tax collection team. That's right: first and foremost, business owners are tax collectors. The government imposes all sorts of requirements on employers to ensure that they not only pay employees correctly but also withhold correctly … and remit those payroll taxes in a timely manner. And if they don't, stiff penalties are assessed against that employer. For this reason, payroll is by far the most commonly outsourced business service, even among companies that don't use a PEO. After all, employees must be paid regularly, and companies that specialize in this can do it much more efficiently than a company can do it for itself. If you are a business owner and you are not outsourcing payroll, you should be!

In addition to paying your employees on time, a payroll company can provide access to elaborate time and attendance systems, prepare your quarterly payroll-tax returns, provide online access to time and payroll records, and process W2s at the end of the year for your employees—all for an additional fee, of course. Technology platforms are constantly evolving, making payroll processing increasingly more efficient for the payroll processor and more accessible and convenient for the client, and there's little doubt that trend will continue. The truth is that when it comes to outsourcing payroll, the choices are endless.

So how is outsourcing payroll to a PEO any different? Well, if we are talking strictly about payroll and its related tax-management services, there is no difference. Sure, some payroll companies are more affordable, while others may have better technology, but they can all do your payroll. What makes a PEO different is the fact that we are not in the payroll business; we are in the people business, and people by necessity expect to be paid. For a PEO, preparing payroll is the mechanism that enables us to deliver many of our more value-centric services. Because we prepare payroll for our clients, their employees have access to a comprehensive suite of benefits that would otherwise be inaccessible to them. And even if our client chooses to retain its own benefits plan, our payroll preparation enables accurate with-holding and documentation for plan eligibility.

Because we prepare payroll for our clients, we maintain records necessary for risk management and workers' compensation coverage. Again, it doesn't matter if the client chooses to participate in our workers' compensation program. Preparing payroll for our clients enables us to provide essential risk-management services. Finally, payroll is an essential mechanism through which unemployment and garnishments are managed. Payroll in and of itself is not the value that PEOs provide clients. Rather, it is a necessary service that enables us to manage all the other more-strategic components of human resources.

Think of payroll like a light switch. When I walk into a dark room, the first thing I do is flip the light switch, and I expect the light to come on. In fact, I take for granted that it will. Once the room is illuminated, I can do whatever I intended to do, because the light makes that possible. If you think about payroll the same way, an employee's paycheck is what enables them to meet life's responsibilities. So in a sense, it makes their lives possible. They expect a certain amount of money to arrive in their bank accounts every week without fail and without errors. They expect the correct amount of taxes to be withheld and properly remitted, and they expect their benefit contributions to be accurately withheld and remitted. Most importantly, they expect an accurate accounting of all this and easy online access to their information. Why not? They should be able to expect this at the very least, just like I expect the light to come on when I flip on the switch.

PEOs are experts at processing payroll, but the true value of the PEO relationship lies in the comprehensiveness of the total package.

If it sounds like I am dismissing the importance of accurate and timely payroll management, I'm not. It is a critically important responsibility, and we take it very seriously; but it is also the most basic and fundamental aspect of being in the PEO business. In fact, if a PEO can't do it and do it well, that PEO won't be in business very long. PEOs are experts at processing payroll, but the true value of the PEO relationship lies in the comprehensiveness of the total package.

PILLAR II: EMPLOYEE BENEFITS

As I've stated throughout this chapter, employees are the lifeblood of any business. And if a business wants to attract and to retain the best and brightest talent, it has to have a competitive benefits plan. Yet for a small company like Joe's, with fifteen employees, the cost is often out of reach. And that cost includes more than just the monthly premium. In fact, the cost of administering a benefits plan can often be more than the cost of the plan itself. Each year, business owners who sponsor employee benefit plans anxiously wait to see what their renewals will look like. Will premiums go up? Will the carrier change the plan design, deductibles, and copays? Will the networks change?

Since the passage of the Affordable Care Act, small-business owners have seen dramatic premium increases that have forced many of them to stop offering health insurance altogether, and those who were committed to maintaining coverages were forced to shop their plans each year. Even with the repeal of the individual mandate in 2019, businesses continue to see their premiums increase each year, along with new ACA-reporting requirements. All of this creates anxiety and stress over the difficult decisions to be made—decisions that can distract a business owner for several weeks at a time. This is where a PEO partnership can really shine, because not only is it able to leverage *economies of scale* to obtain lower rates but it is also able to offer multiple plan designs that allow each employee to choose the plan best suited for their individual circumstances. Most PEOs have a full suite of benefits options, which include major medical plans with Health Savings Account (HSA) and Flexible Spending Account (FSA) options. PEOs provide access to an assortment of voluntary benefits, which are specifically tailored to the employee's individual needs, and these programs are managed to take advantage of section-125 pretax deductions (often referred to as a "cafeteria plan"). PEOs also manage the time-consuming open-enrollment process, answering employee questions and explaining the various options.

In fact, through a PEO partnership, the employees of small businesses gain access to *all* big-business employee benefits, such as 401(k) plans; health, dental, life, and other insurances; dependent care; and other benefits they might not typically receive as employees of a small company. Studies conducted by NAPEO show that only 27 percent of small businesses offer employee retirement plans (according to the NFIB), while approximately *95 percent* of NAPEO members offer retirement plans to their employees. And more than that, virtually all of those offer some level of matching contribution.[6]

So from a benefits perspective, PEOs offer small businesses incredible opportunities that would otherwise be out of reach.

PILLAR III: SAFETY AND RISK MANAGEMENT

If you ask a small-business owner what poses the greatest threat to their business, you are likely to get a variety of answers. While it's true that today's small-business owner faces risks on many fronts, for many, being held financially liable for something over which they have little direct control is likely at the top of the list. But does this idea apply to workplace safety? How much control can a business owner truly have? Well, for a PEO, the ability to effectively manage this risk can determine its very survival. When a PEO enrolls a new client, the PEO is accepting the risk associated with that client's operations. So you can bet your bottom dollar that the PEO is going to investigate and underwrite every potential exposure. If a company has industrial exposures, which includes any working environment with active moving machinery, it needs to have a written safety

---

6   National Association of Professional Employment Organizations, *Facts about Professional Employment Organizations (PEOs)*, 2014, https://www.napeo.org/docs/default-source/Member-Resources/peo-fact-sheet-12-8-2015573145ac2ab-0647c9e4fff00004fd204.pdf.

program. In fact, most workers' compensation carriers require this as a prerequisite to coverage!

Many small businesses have a certain level of risk baked right into their business models. Take the construction industry, for example, with its extremely heavy equipment and vehicles, all sorts of specialized and dangerous machinery, and on top of it all, the necessity to operate in high-risk environments. As you might imagine, that industry is not very popular among workers' compensation carriers, due to the potential for claims. Builders, electricians, manufacturers—just about any industry which has an industrial component automatically comes with an increased degree of risk. Yet many small businesses that have a clear exposure to employee injury do not have any formalized risk-management programs in place. That's exactly why the construction industry and others like it turn to PEOs to assist with all their risk-management needs.

PEOs help their clients develop effective safety programs. During the underwriting phase, a PEO will determine the prospective client's current risk profile, by studying claims history and reviewing the company's NCCI (National Council on Compensation Insurance) experience-rating trend. Most importantly, industrial exposures require a site visit, so that operations can be observed and key people can be interviewed. Depending on the outcome of this underwriting, a decision is made whether the prospective client qualifies for the PEO's master workers' compensation policy or if the client will need to be on a separate policy of their own. If the company's risk requires some degree of rehabilitation, the PEO can still enroll the company as a client but will likely want to cover the client on a policy written in the company's name. This is called a "carve-out" policy, because the new client is not a part of the PEO's master policy. The carve-out policy is usually at a higher rate than the PEO's master policy. Why?

Because the PEO's master policy is reserved for those clients whose risk profile does not pose a disproportionately higher risk to the overall plan. This is when the PEO's true risk-management begins. The goal is to work with the client to rehabilitate the risk through proactive safety engineering, so that the client can soon benefit from the savings of being on the PEO's master policy.

It's important to understand why every client isn't automatically accepted into the PEO's master policy. For one, the master policy is deeply discounted because the PEO is either self-funding or has accepted a high retention level. It is only by controlling claims costs that clients in the master policy receive value in the form of discounted rates. Allowing clients into the master policy before their risks have been rehabilitated has the potential to drive claims frequency and cost up, which would increase the cost for every client in the plan.

As challenging as managing worksite risk is, it was made exponentially more difficult by the COVID-19 crisis. When the pandemic first hit, risk managers around the country received very little guidance from OSHA, and they were unsure how the NCCI would assess infections. Would infections be treated as workplace recordable incidents, and how could the source of an infected worker's contamination be proved or disproved? Initially, OSHA did not consider virus-related illnesses to be work-related, so they were not recordable. However, as the pandemic progressed, OSHA changed its position and began designating infections incurred by workers in "frontline" professions, like healthcare and delivery, to be work-related and therefore recordable. But as the pandemic continued to rage, OSHA, in an attempt to cover all bases, released revised guidance suggesting that any workplace could potentially be responsible for work-related exposure to the virus. This guidance, which is the most current as of this writing, requires an employer to conduct an investigation, which may or may not result in the employer being held responsible. The truth is, whether employers will be held responsible for certain COVID-19 infections is unknown and could depend on the state. As of this writing, lawsuits are being filed on behalf of infected workers, and Congress is debating whether employers should be held responsible for or protected from COVID-19-related liability. Whatever is decided by Congress, PEO safety professionals will be right there monitoring developments and advising their clients.

At Lyons HR, we have a whole team of people in our risk department whose sole responsibility is to identify risks and to develop meaningful safety plans at the work sites of our clients. These safety professionals stay on top of the regulations for risk mitigation and safety compliance. As a result, not only does a small business that partners with a PEO have a much safer work environment, but actuarial data shows that PEOs aggressively manage workers' compensation risks and reduce the basic costs of workers' compensation by as much as 25 percent for small businesses.[7]

PILLAR IV: HR COMPLIANCE

Many new PEO clients, who were originally attracted to the relationship by lower health insurance or workers' compensation costs, soon breathe a sigh of relief when they discover how out of compliance they previously were. Ask any PEO operator, and they will tell you the most critical component to the PEO value proposition is the often-overlooked area of human-resource management and compliance. Unlike payroll, which is considered by some to be a

---

7   Ibid.

commodity component of the service, HR compliance demands ongoing monitoring and consultative feedback regarding the most important yet variable asset of any company: its people. And unlike more-immediate cost savings associated with health or workers' compensation premiums, the savings associated with HR compliance can take time to be realized. But in the long run, these are by far the most valuable.

Earlier in this book I talked about the myriad of employment laws and regulations that have been passed through the years. All the different acronyms that refer to these laws are often referred to as the "alphabet soup of HR." It's enough to make your head explode. On one hand, to grow the economy, the government encourages entrepreneurship and the innovation of small businesses to serve the masses in various industries. But on the other hand, agencies of the government enforce all sorts of burdens, regulations, restrictions, obligations, and responsibilities on any employer who has more than one employee. And as demonstrated over the past few decades, governmental agencies are only going to become more and more intrusive in the inner workings of businesses, so it stands to reason that over time, that list of regulations and responsibilities is going to continue to get longer and longer.

I talked about risk management in the previous section, but a company's employment practices represent an even greater potential risk that needs to be mitigated. Companies that partner with a PEO give themselves an extra layer of insulation from employment liability through the coemployer relationship. Some PEOs, as is the case with Lyons HR, extend their Employment Practices Liability Insurance (EPLI) coverage to their clients, saving them the cost of maintaining their own separate EPLI policies. This also gives the PEO an even greater incentive to ensure the client remains compliant, because the PEO is now sharing in the liability of its client's employment practices. The sharing of these liabilities can vary and is specifically defined in the Client Service Agreement, but the mitigation of this liability is another reason why HR compliance is the most critical component of the value proposition.

The workplace is a melting pot of liability for employers. Are your hiring practices lawful? What about your compensation plan? Is it discriminatory? What about terminations? Do you have all the bases covered? How do you determine when an employee deserves a promotion or a raise? The potential liability for stepping on one of these landmines is huge!

One of the first things a PEO will do with any new client is update the company's job descriptions and employee handbook. Many times, a new client will have neither, in which case they are created from scratch. Although these documents are specifically customized to the client, they will always contain legally required provisions. We have found that any time a client becomes involved with employment-related litigation, usually the first items of discovery requested by the plaintiff's attorney are the company's handbook and the employee's job description. The plaintiff's attorneys will scrub these documents thoroughly, in hopes of finding a policy that violates a prevailing law, so employers need to be prepared. It is critical that these two important documents be maintained accurately and legally.

So to summarize, the most compelling reason for a small business to partner with a PEO is not because the PEO is efficient at processing payroll or because it can lower the business's insurance costs. Rather, it is the PEO's comprehensive understanding of the increasing complexity and legal responsibilities of being an employer and its ability to keep its clients compliant.

Compared to employees working in businesses that are not PEO clients, employees working in businesses that are PEO clients are significantly more likely to report the following:[8]

- Their employers demonstrate a commitment to them as employees, resulting in higher job satisfaction.

- Their employers have a more thorough hiring process.

- Their employers have effective HR policies and practices that promote employee loyalty.

- Their employers provide training and career-development opportunities.

Employees of PEO clients also report significantly higher scores on key measures related to employee satisfaction and confidence in company management:[9]

- Levels of employee engagement

- Intention to stay with their current employer until retirement

- Belief that their employer is taking the right steps to be competitive

- Trust that their employer is supporting employees in delivering excellent customer service

- Confidence in their employer's approach to growing the company

---

8   Laurie Bassi and Dan McMurrer, "PEOs: Good for Businesses and Their Employees," *NAPEO White Paper Series* no. 5 (September 2017), https://www. napeo.org/docs/default-source/white-papers/2017-napeo-white-paper-final.pdf.

9   Ibid.

A TEAM OF EXPERTS ON YOUR SIDE

Think about all the vendors the typical business must engage just to have employees. Health-insurance brokers, workers' compensation brokers, attorneys, CPAs, 401(k)-plan administrators, providers of time and attendance systems—the list goes on. Outside of a PEO relationship, all those vendors are disconnected from each other and in many cases don't even know each other. The business receives a separate invoice for each, with little if any system-wide integration. Doesn't it make more sense for all these critical employee functions to be managed on the same technology platform by a team of experts who know your business and are in constant communication with each other? No matter what a small-business owner's employment-related issue might be, with a PEO on their side, they have a robust team of subject-matter experts to call upon for help.

> No matter what a small-business owner's employment-related issue might be, with a PEO on their side, they have a robust team of subject-matter experts to call upon for help.

Take our auto-repair shop owner, Joe, for example. By signing up with a PEO, if he has an issue regarding benefits for his employees, he instantly has a benefits expert at his fingertips. If his problem is with OSHA or safety compliance, then he has a dedicated risk manager whom he can call to assist him through the problem step by step. If Joe's wife, Judy, has a question or concern about payroll taxes, she has a tax expert at the PEO who can help walk her through it. Or if Joe has a question regarding employment policy and procedure, then he has an HR professional he can call. Any single issue that touches an employee, Joe has resources and support from his PEO—resources that most small-business owners could never afford to have on staff. But with a PEO, suddenly that small business can harness the same power as a major corporation and compete at a much higher level.

PEO COST ANALYSIS

Of all the motivations that may drive a small business toward a relationship with a PEO, at the end of the day they all boil down to one unavoidable sticking point: cost.

For all of the HR services provided—to have a team of experts just a phone call or email away, to have access to great benefits, and to reclaim time, energy, and peace of mind—the cost of hiring a PEO must be outrageous and well beyond the means of most small businesses! This is what many business owners who are unfamiliar with PEOs often think. Well, think again! A PEO relationship can usually be acquired at a fraction of what it would cost to hire a single HR employee, let alone a team of experts in various areas.

Allow me to illustrate with a hypothetical scenario. Let's say Roger is the owner of a small IT company, consisting of twenty-five employees who each make $50,000 per year. That translates to $1,250,000 in payroll every year. A run-of-the-mill, out-of-the-box PEO service might price Roger's IT company at an annual rate of $1,000 per employee to deliver all four Pillars of Profitability. Let's do the math: twenty-five employees multiplied by $1,000 equals $25,000 per year in management fees.

Now if Roger were looking to spend that same amount of money and hire an HR person for his company, when you allow for the payroll tax and cost of benefits for this person, their salary would be around $21,600 per year. Divide that by the standard 2,080 work hours each year, and we have $10.38 per hour. What kind of experience and expertise do you think Roger can hire for $10.38 an hour? Someone who has risk-management and EEOC labor experience? Someone who can handle his payroll and do all of his payroll-tax filings on time?

Granted, some PEOs may charge more or less than others, depending on what a client's needs are, but even if a PEO quoted Roger a rate of $1,200 per employee, the value gained far exceeds the money expended.

Another service that PEOs offer and charge for is a client's participation in the PEO's master workers' compensation plan. So let's say that the PEO Roger is considering has a master plan with a $250,000 deductible. The PEO is assuming a considerable amount of risk, but if the PEO is willing to take on the risk associated with Roger's IT company, then the PEO will provide coverage at a discounted rate that Roger would never have access to on his own. For example, if the class code for Roger's industry is $2.00 per $100.00 in payroll, by going with the PEO, Roger now might be getting a rate of $1.20 per $100.00 in payroll. This would result in an annual premium for his twenty-five employees of $15,000, compared to an annual premium of $25,000 without going through the PEO.

At this point, the PEO may build a small margin into the rate it quotes to Roger, for two reasons. First, the PEO is assuming the risk of the deductible. Secondly, the PEO is assuming responsibility for administration of all costs of claims, as well as anything else that may take place. So whereas the PEO is given a rate from the carrier of $1.20, it may charge Roger the $1.20 plus a claims management fee of $0.30, for a total cost to Roger of $1.50. This is still a 25 percent discount from what he would otherwise pay.

— In this example, the PEO is allowing $3,750 to implement safety procedures and to manage safety and risk at Roger's location. It will also administer and investigate any claims that may come up. And it will cover any and all deductibles—which may or may not be billed back to the client.

— The third way that a PEO can earn margin is through the effective management of SUTA, the State Unemployment Tax Act. As explained earlier in the book, every state has its own SUTA rates, which are based on a small business's experience with former employees filing unemployment claims. The more turnover a company has, the higher their SUTA rate is going to be. So a PEO is going to be extremely diligent in managing SUTA claims to make sure it keeps the SUTA rate as low as it possibly can.

— For example, let's assume that Roger's SUTA rate is 2.5 percent, because he's had a couple of unemployment claims recently. But the PEO has a SUTA rate of 1.5 percent. The SUTA wage base in Roger's state is $7,000. So for Roger, if we take $7,000 and multiply it by twenty-five employees, we have $175,000 worth of payroll that will be taxed for SUTA. That means that Roger would pay $4,375 in SUTA taxes while the PEO would pay $2,625 to the state on behalf of Roger to insure those same employees. Yet the PEO is likely going to bill Roger not at 1.5 percent, but 1.8 percent, creating an arbitrage of $525. And for that $525, the PEO will answer any and all unemployment inquiries, investigate all unemployment claims, attend hearings, and defend Roger's company if there is a disputed claim.

That's an awfully large return on investment for $525!

How do these #'s compare

THE TIPPING POINT

When you look at the margin for Roger's PEO—the annual administration fees of $25,000, the workers' compensation arbitrage of $3,750, and the SUTA arbitrage of $525—you can see that Roger is paying $29,275 per year to the PEO, but he is saving money on his workers' compensation premium and his SUTA taxes and is receiving the benefit of a full HR team of experts at his fingertips. Consider the fact that hiring just one qualified, experienced HR professional on staff could easily cost Roger $80,000–$90,000 or more with salary, payroll taxes, and benefits, and it becomes even clearer what a tremendous deal Roger is getting.

So the very basic question that any small-business owner has to ask themselves when considering a relationship with a PEO is this: "Am I better off to go out and hire an HR professional or to use a PEO and take advantage of its systems, buying power, and economies of scale?"

This answer changes as a small business grows. As our example with Roger illustrates, a relationship with a PEO for twenty-five employees costs Roger roughly $29,000 per year. What if he has fifty employees? All factors being equal, we can assume it would cost him around $58,000 per year. Clearly Roger is still getting a great deal. Let's double his growth to one hundred employees. Now he's paying over $116,000 to the PEO each year, slightly more than it might cost to hire his own HR professional. This begins the tipping point for many small businesses, which is why the PEO industry typically targets companies in the fifteen- to one-hundred-employee range.

Yet even at that point, is Roger really better off with a single HR professional on staff, compared to a team of experts who will never call in sick or take off for Hawaii in August? A case can easily be made that unless a small business has the capabilities to hire an entire HR department, the better value in the long run is that relationship with the PEO. With a PEO, a small business has a team of HR experts who are highly skilled in risk management, in workers' compensation and risk management, in evaluating benefit plans, and in payroll taxes and tax administration.

As the PEO industry has evolved over the years, small-business owners all over the nation, like Joe and Roger, have begun to realize the benefits of a PEO partnership. But it wasn't until 2014 that the industry would see an explosion of growth—and the much sought-after legal certainty from the federal government—which said to the world that PEOs were here to stay.

PEO INDUSTRY SPOTLIGHT

DALE HAGEMAN

It is often said that CPAs with a background in financial management make good PEO operators, and that is certainly true in the case of Dale Hageman. After spending his early years in public accounting, Hageman took his finance and accounting skills into private industry. In 1982, he became chief financial officer for a large property-management firm in Oklahoma City. In addition to managing the firm's finances, Hageman was responsible for human resources, employee payroll, employee benefits, and risk management, which included insurance procurement. Over time he developed a proprietary system for capturing all employee-related costs. These costs were then charged in the form of fees to properties under management.

In 1992, Hageman used his experience to establish Accord Human Resources, a PEO based in Oklahoma City. From a single office with only four employees, Hageman grew Accord into the largest PEO in Oklahoma, working with hundreds of client companies and thousands of worksite employees across the country.

"Those first couple of years were slow," Hageman recalls. "The only option we had for workers' compensation insurance was the Oklahoma State Insurance Fund. They imposed a costly 1.75 percent modifier (surcharge) on all new PEOs. But once we were able to secure coverage with a major carrier, our business really took off. The business grew because we had some truly great people who were committed to our clients. Our high client and employee retention were a testament to the kind of culture we were able to create."

Hageman has been a tireless advocate for the advancement of PEOs during his career. In 2002, he was a key contributor to the National Association of Professional Employer Organizations (NAPEO) state PEO Model Act, which was similarly adopted by Oklahoma, New York, and other states around the country. In the early 1990s, Hageman teamed up with other industry leaders in Texas to resolve a dispute with the Texas Employment Commission. This dispute was ultimately resolved with the commission, allowing PEOs to be the employers of record for unemployment purposes. Hageman has been an active member and past chairman of the boards of both PEO-industry associations: Professional Administrative Co-Employers (PACE) and NAPEO. As a CPA and entrepreneur, Hageman has been a respected leader in the Oklahoma City business community for almost forty years.

He has been recognized for his civic contributions, his contributions to the field of accounting, and his contributions to the advancement of the PEO industry at both state and national levels.

When Accord Human Resources was acquired by TriNet in 2012, Hageman remained with the company for two years to assist with transition and integration. During that period he also consulted as a business strategist with entrepreneurs across the country. In September of 2015, Hageman launched his second PEO, Spirit Human Resources, where he serves as CEO.

"I've dedicated my career to helping companies grow and succeed. Providing services through a PEO is the best way I can do that. The industry has made great strides since I started in 1992, and I believe the future is bright. The ever-increasing complexity of being an employer, along with the availability of capital and advancements in technology, will continue to drive growth in the industry."

CHAPTER FIVE

2014–A GIANT LEAP FORWARD

All progress takes place outside our comfort zone.
—Michael John Bobak

J oe was crunching the numbers. After being introduced to the idea of using a PEO by his friend Dan, Joe had spent the following weeks researching the industry and trying to decide if a PEO was right for him. How, after fifteen years in business, had he never heard of one? When he considered all the services offered by PEOs and the amount of burden that could be taken off him, he began to wonder how much he could grow his business if he could focus all his attention on recruiting and training mechanics, opening new locations, and promoting his business brand. Joe's Auto Repair was already the preferred shop in town, so it was clear that Joe knew how to fix cars and train mechanics.

I could even franchise my business and open Joe's Auto Repair franchises all over the country, Joe thought to himself. The growth possibilities were endless, and Joe was getting excited.

Being completely unfamiliar with the concept of coemployment, Joe read all he could to educate himself on it. He was particularly intrigued by the sharing of employment liabilities and by the way PEOs aggregate insurance products. After completing his due diligence and exploring dozens of websites, Joe eventually contacted the PEO that Dan was using. After all, his friend had highly recommended it. Joe was eager to learn how it would address the problems he had experienced with employee turnover and the increasing cost of health insurance. Like other entrepreneurs across the country, Joe had been following the national news surrounding the Affordable Care Act and hearing about how it would impact small businesses like his. For the past fifteen years, Joe had struggled to provide health insurance to his employees; now, with the nation's attention focused on the issue, Joe felt confident that obtaining coverage through a PEO was his best option.

THE AFFORDABLE CARE ACT

The Patient Protection and Affordable Care Act (ACA) technically passed in March of 2010, but it took nearly four years to finally take effect due to political infighting and several failed attempts to repeal it. But when it did finally become the law of the land, the ACA quickly became one of the biggest drivers of small businesses to the PEO industry, because the ACA created so much confusion. It was a massive piece of legislation that changed the way we viewed healthcare in this country. It introduced new terms and phrases like "pay or play," "minimum essential coverage," and "Cadillac tax," along with the intimidating employer mandate. Business owners had many questions, but the question I remember hearing the most was about how the state exchanges would work. Would a business owner be better off not sponsoring a health plan and just encouraging their employees to get coverage through the exchanges?

Because there were four years between the ACA's passage and its eventual enactment, PEOs made it a priority to learn and understand the new law. We knew business owners would have difficult decisions to make, and it was important that we be able to advise them. I remember reading everything I could and closely following the contentious debate about the public mandate. Accompanying the law itself was an intricate regulatory framework. All this complexity, along with the new ACA-reporting requirements, created a profound opportunity for the industry. And as expected, there was a tsunami of inquiries from new PEO prospects.

Small-business owners like Joe, who had been riding the healthcare fence for years, decided it would be much easier to outsource the stress and responsibility to the health-insurance experts at a PEO rather than try to make sense of all the ACA provisions by themselves. In fact, the anxiety associated with the ACA and all the confusing mandates created one of the largest surges in the PEO industry—nearly 25 percent growth in 2014 alone.

No matter which direction you lean politically, there is no question that the enactment of the Affordable Care Act in 2014 forever changed the landscape of health insurance in this country. Yet 2014 would also see another major development for the PEO industry, bookended in December by the passing of the Small Business Efficiency Act.

THE SMALL BUSINESS EFFICIENCY ACT

The one thing the PEO industry had always lacked was federal leg-islation validating the concept of the business model itself. But after seventeen years of lobbying by NAPEO and others, the passing of the Small Business Efficiency Act (SBEA) represented a watershed moment for the PEO industry. Whereas all previous legislation having to do with labor viewed alternative-employment arrange-ments as an afterthought, this was the one piece of legislation that had been specifically written for the industry.

The big advantage of the SBEA was the fact that it gave legal certainty at the federal level to the industry and removed all of those questions and concerns that people had for years about engaging in a relationship with a PEO:

Is a PEO obligated to remit my payroll taxes? What happens if it doesn't? What about the employer tax credits that are available to me as the employer? If I run my employees through the PEO, do I lose those tax credits?

All those lingering questions were finally answered by the passing of this legislation, and it began with a new IRS voluntary certification process.

IRS CERTIFICATION

The voluntary certification program offered a new minimum level of assurance for the PEO industry. I'm proud to say that Lyons HR was among the first ten PEOs in the country to become certified by the IRS, and I can say with absolute confidence it was a very rigorous process. PEOs looking to get certified must have thorough background checks on all controlling persons—essentially anyone who is in a position of authority. Next, the PEO must submit financial statements, meet certain liquidity ratios, and post a bond. Beyond that, it must provide an audit and comply with all requirements on an ongoing basis.

Here is a full list of requirements a PEO must fulfill to obtain IRS certification, according to NAPEO:[10]

- Bonding: A certified PEO must maintain a $50,000 bond, or a bond in an amount that is equal to 5 percent of the PEO's federal employment tax liabilities, if they were greater than $50,000 for the previous year (not to exceed $1 million).

- Annual audits: A certified PEO must prepare and provide the IRS with annual independent financial-statement audits prepared by a CPA.

- Quarterly CPA attestations on employment taxes: A certified PEO must provide quarterly assertions to the IRS regarding payment of all employment taxes, accompanied by an examination-level attestation by an independent CPA with respect to each such assertion.

- Annual fee: The certified PEO must pay an annual fee of up to $1,000 per year to be (and remain) certified.

- Inclusion in published list of CPEOs: The IRS will publish a list of all certified PEOs (CPEOs), as well as a list of those PEOs whose certification has been revoked or suspended.

- Certified PEO sole liability: The certified PEO assumes sole liability for the collection and remission of federal payroll taxes with respect to wages paid by the certified PEO to worksite employees. A worksite employee is an individual

---

10   National Association of Professional Employment Organizations, *What Does the Small Business Efficiency Act (SBEA) Mean for the PEO Industry?*, 2014, https://napeo.blob.core.windows.net/cdn/docs/default-source/SBEA-Documents/sbea-factsheetfebruary2015.pdf.

who performs services for a customer at a qualifying worksite under a qualifying service contract between such customer and the certified PEO.

Now let's unpack some of the provisions of the certification process to better understand how the SBEA was a true game changer for the PEO industry.

PEOS RECOGNIZED UNDER FEDERAL TAX LAW

With this aspect of the law enacted, PEOs finally had the opportunity to step out from the dark shadow that had been cast by their

> **With this aspect of the law enacted, PEOs finally had the opportunity to step out from the dark shadow that had been cast by their less-than-righteous predecessors, who had collected payroll taxes from their clients and had run off in the night, leaving them with unpaid tax liabilities.**

less-than-righteous predecessors, who had collected payroll taxes from their clients and had run off in the night, leaving them with unpaid tax liabilities. Now, a PEO that chooses to be certified, becoming a CPEO, would have clear statutory authority to collect and remit federal employment taxes under the CPEO's EIN for wages the CPEO pays to worksite employees. This is more than just the authority to collect and remit, however; it is a *legal liability* to do so. So if the PEO for whatever reason elects not to pay its client's taxes, that PEO would now be held liable, not the client. And not only is the PEO responsible for remitting its client's taxes, but it also must do so regardless of whether it collects it from the client.

This provision alone offered a whole new level of security for many small businesses considering a relationship with a PEO.

ELIMINATION OF WAGE RESTARTS

One of the benefits of the SBEA that was a huge deal for CPEOs was extending the sales cycle to a full twelve months, a departure from the previous two-month, cram-it-all-in-at-the-end-of-the-year cycle. The way it used to work, FICA and FUTA wage bases would restart when a client joined or left a PEO midyear, so everyone would wait until the end of the year to sign on with a PEO.

For example, the FICA wage base is $137,700 for the year 2020, which means the first $137,700 of wages for every employee is taxed at 6.2 percent, or a max of $8,537. Employers also pay 0.6 percent on the first $7,000 in wages for FUTA taxes. But if it's June or July, chances are that most employees have already hit their FUTA limit and have also made significant contributions toward the FICA wage base. Most small-business owners therefore were reluctant to get into a PEO relationship in the middle of the year and would rather just wait until the beginning of the next tax year before considering a PEO relationship. This was one of the primary reasons most PEOs developed an ASO offering. They were able to onboard new companies as ASO clients in the middle of the year, then convert them into PEO clients on January 1, when the wage base started over.

But with the passing of the SBEA, certified PEOs are considered to be a successor employer to their client and therefore no longer have to worry about wage-base restarts. This was significant because it opened the opportunity for certified PEOs to sign on new clients all year round. It is important to point out that this successor employer status is not granted to PEOs that are not certified by the IRS.

RETAINING TAX CREDITS

The federal tax code provides for tax credits to employers who pay wages to certain targeted groups and for wages associated with activities the government wants to incentivize. This includes wages incurred in predefined research-and-development activities as well as in clinical testing for new vaccines. But the most common credits are the work-opportunity tax credit and the empowerment-zone credit, which are both designed to incentivize employers to hire people from historically disadvantaged groups. Prior to the passing of the SBEA, there was a genuine concern among clients who qualified for one or more of these credits that paying wages through a PEO could potentially render them ineligible for the credit. As the statutory employer for the purposes of payroll, employee wages are reported under the PEO's federal identification number, so the client effectively reports zero wages in the eyes of the IRS. That's a real problem when a company is trying to take advantage of one of these credits.

Legislators must have listened to the concerns of the industry when drafting the SBEA, because the final version of the act included specific language that identified the client company, not the PEO, as the entity entitled to federal tax credits associated with any qualifying wages paid through the PEO. A certified PEO must provide the client company with all the information needed to apply for these credits. By contrast, if a PEO is not certified, determining the party that is eligible for these tax credits can get complicated and is unlikely to remain consistent among the available credits.

A NEW ERA

There is little doubt that the SBEA and ACA will continue to have a profound impact on the PEO industry. The passage of the SBEA certainly gave existing PEO clients greater comfort if their PEO was certified, but moreover it helped the PEO industry expand into virgin accounts. If the value propositions for small businesses signing on with a PEO were strong before, now they were virtually bulletproof ... that is, as long as the PEO devoted the time and resources to become certified.

Remember, none of the advantages listed in this chapter apply to noncertified PEOs, which unfortunately make up a majority of the industry. In fact, according to Bradley S. Buttermore's 2015 article in *PEO Insider*, "not being certified will likely put a PEO at a disadvantage compared to certified competitors because certification requirements will be perceived as a measure of professional expertise, credibility, and financial strength."[11]

> **If the value propositions for small businesses signing on with a PEO were strong before, now they were virtually bulletproof ... that is, as long as the PEO devoted the time and resources to become certified.**

Couple that with the fact that certification is a rigorous process with ongoing compliance requirements and costs, and that could put a real strain on boutique PEOs, forcing them either to merge or close up shop due to an inability to compete.

Which leads us to the notion ... not all PEOs are created equal.

---

11   Bradley Buttermore, "The Impact of the SBEA on the PEO Industry," *PEO Insider*, November 2015, 41.

PEO INDUSTRY SPOTLIGHT

BRENT TILSON

Some people are born entrepreneurs and seem able to make just about any business they pursue successful. Brent Tilson is just such an entrepreneur. Tilson began his career with the accounting firm, KMPG (Klynveld Peat Marwick Goerdeler) International Cooperative, before establishing B. R. Tilson & Company, CPAs, in 1992. But it wasn't until Tilson was approached by a medical-staffing firm about providing payroll-management services for 250 physical therapists that Tilson had the idea of starting his own PEO. After researching the industry, he recognized the market opportunity, and Tilson HR was established in 1995. From its early existence, Tilson HR attracted many white-collar companies and resulted in a much higher average annual salary per employee. Unlike some PEOs, who cater to a more industrial blue-collar workforce, Tilson's business model was not based on risk arbitrage, so his company was essentially unaffected by periods of hardening insurance markets. Tilson's business philosophy was a success, and the company grew.

Tilson recalled a particularly pivotal moment in his company's history, which occurred around 2004 when a large technology client terminated services. The reason given for the termination was that it had "outgrown" his PEO. Determined to never let that happen again, Tilson began developing his scalable HR-services model, which defines the company's service model today. Tilson created an HR-capability-transfer model that integrates flexible HR best practices and web-based information technology. This model is described more fully in Tilson's book, *Go Slow to Grow Fast*, published by ForbesBooks in 2018.

As an operator, NAPEO board member, and tireless industry advocate, Tilson has experienced it all in the PEO business. But perhaps his greatest contributions to the industry occurred during the critical passage of the SBEA in 2014. I asked him what it was like to be the NAPEO chairman when this landmark legislation finally passed.

"Every NAPEO chairman before me had made achieving federal recognition their number one initiative," Tilson said. "And now, after twenty years of hard work from NAPEO members and staff, the moment had finally arrived. I vividly remember the phone call I received from NAPEO president, Pat Cleary. His first words were 'Hey buddy, pour yourself a drink. The bill just got dropped ... it looks like this is finally going to happen.' Our celebration was short-lived, because we knew once the bill became law, the real work would begin. We immediately began to strategize because there were opponents who did not like the bill. I recall a small group of us sitting in a conference room inside the US Treasury Building with representatives from the IRS, who were not exactly thrilled to be meeting with us. They made it clear that they had not advocated for the new law and were not happy about the dedicated resources that would be required to implement it. But we were determined to make the most of this opportunity, so we worked diligently with our outside counsel and with the IRS to make certain the provisions in the final tax code accurately reflected the intent of the legislation."

Over the next year, the structure for the SBEA was crafted into IRC Section 3511, which also established the PEO Certification program.

Tilson continues to play a key role in the advancement of the PEO industry and is often a featured speaker at industry events.

"I was especially proud of how the industry stepped up during the COVID-19 pandemic to help clients navigate the intricate provisions of the CARES Act," Tilson said. "Although technology-based Managed Services Platforms continue to evolve, the way PEOs around the country have served their clients speaks to the level of dedication we all have to our clients, and you can't replace that with software."

CHAPTER SIX

NOT ALL PEOS ARE CREATED EQUAL

It takes twenty years to build a reputation and five minutes to ruin it. If you think about that, you'll do things differently.

—Warren Buffett

Joe's Auto Repair is thriving! Since partnering with his PEO the year before, Joe is planning to recruit three new technicians to staff another location he's establishing in a growing part of town. Joe is thankful that his wife, Judy, no longer has to prepare the weekly payroll or be burdened by all her other employee responsibilities at the shop. Instead, she is now able to spend more time at home, attending to their growing family. And if Judy is needed for anything, the HR information system (HRIS) the PEO has implemented is accessible from anywhere, 24-7. The system is easy to use and provides everything they need to know about their employees all in one place, accessible with just a few clicks.

Joe was surprised to learn that many of his old employment practices were not exactly compliant with current Department of Labor regulations. Joe had not always followed the DOL Wage and Hour Division's guidelines, and he was always confused about who was exempt from overtime. Fortunately, the PEO conducted a complete internal HR audit and created a customized employee handbook, which made several HR-policy corrections. Joe considered himself lucky that his previous practices had never been legally challenged, and he was relieved to know that he would no longer be taking that risk. In addition to legally required policy content, the PEO made several other HR-policy recommendations, which Joe enthusiastically embraced. One was a flextime work schedule that was designed to reduce absenteeism and turnover, and another was a new vacation policy and PTO plan, which would be meticulously tracked through the new HRIS database. Employee morale at Joe's Auto Repair is at an all-time high!

Joe is glad that HR is finally being managed the right way, but he is also a dollars-and-cents kind of guy. Because of the new written safety program that Joe's PEO has implemented over the past year, he is now saving 25 percent on his workers' compensation insurance cost. And the pay-as-you-go premium plan made available through his PEO means there will be no surprise audit premium at the end of the policy period. This is a big relief to Joe, because as his business has grown, so has his payroll expense, and that always meant a huge audit premium at the end of the policy year. The PEO's risk professionals also conduct periodic reviews with Joe to ensure the program remains as effective as it can be.

The PEO is managing Joe's payroll and payroll taxes; it has installed a comprehensive compliant HR infrastructure; and it has implemented a written safety program that is saving Joe thousands in workers' compensation costs. But what excites Joe the most is being able to finally provide affordable health insurance to his employees. This had always been a problem in the past and had caused Joe to lose some very talented technicians over the years. Now, finally, through the buying power of his PEO, Joe is able to offer a flexible suite of benefits that he never thought would be possible. Joe's profits are soaring, because he has solved the turnover problem that had plagued him for years.

Joe's journey to working with a PEO is very common in that most new PEO clients are the result of a referral from a trusted friend or professional advisor. Joe and Dan's experience should be very similar, since they are both working with the same PEO, but there are differences in PEOs that need to be understood. To be considered a PEO under the legal definition, a PEO must provide to some degree the four Pillars of Profitability described earlier: (1) Payroll and Payroll-Tax Administration, (2) Employee Benefits, (3) Safety and Risk Management, and (4) HR Compliance. And as you well know by now, a small business's relationship with any PEO is a coemployment relationship, which means that the client is the common-law employer and the PEO is the statutory employer.

But there are a myriad of ways PEOs go about serving their clients' needs. And depending on the size of a PEO, the region of the country it services, the industries it has experience with, and dozens of other factors, it's a fair statement to say that no two PEOs are exactly alike. Here we'll dig a little deeper into some of those factors to see what creates the differences between one PEO and another, beginning with one of the biggest drivers of the industry …

HEALTH-INSURANCE PLANS

Access to affordable health insurance is only one component of the PEO value proposition, but it's a big one. It is the search for affordable health insurance that most often leads small-business owners to discover PEOs in the first place. But when it comes to how PEOs deliver health insurance to their employees, there are differences that need to be understood.

First and foremost, the Affordable Care Act forever changed healthcare in this country. Most significant were the imposed mandates on larger employers with more than fifty full-time employees, the establishment of a federally subsidized health market for low-income citizens, and the availability of tax credits for smaller employers through the Small Business Health Options Program (SHOP). But the objective of the ACA was not to make conducting business in the United States easier. Far from it! Its objective was to increase affordable access to healthcare for previously uninsured workers by imposing sweeping new requirements onto employers. Today, there are a whole host of options available for individuals and small businesses through the HealthCare.gov marketplace. In this healthcare environment, if a small business is solely going out there looking for the best rate, it may very well find it itself on the exchange.

But here's the problem: rates aren't everything in a health-insurance policy.

Cost and value are very different concepts. This may seem obvious, but it's easy to get swept up in comparing monthly premium costs without taking all of the other policy aspects into consideration.

There are endless plan designs that aren't always clearly understood when a small-business owner is scouring the marketplace looking for the best rate. Unless they are comparing features—deductibles, inpatient care, outpatient care, referral requirements, network specifications, vision benefits, prescription coverages, and copays—the rate is arbitrary. The fact is that it's very hard to compare health plans across different carriers, because there are so many variables. That's where a PEO relationship can really help small-business owners.

Healthcare options offered by PEOs can vary greatly. For example, the largest PEOs in the country are likely to have a master health plan with more than one major health-insurance carrier, and those plans are almost certainly self-funded. By that, I mean claims are paid not by the insurance carrier, but by the PEO, who is the plan sponsor. Self-funded plans have been around for years and are popular with larger employers for several reasons. Unlike community-rated guaranteed-cost plans, self-funded plans offer more flexibility in plan design and are not subject to state regulations or state premium tax, which is a huge advantage. Large PEOs with thousands of employees can do the same thing, but the fiduciary responsibility associated with sponsoring a self-funded plan is enormous, and it is critical that the PEO doesn't use artificially low premiums to lure in new clients. For this reason, PEOs will usually partner with a healthcare consultant or actuarial firm that can study the census and properly underwrite the risk to make certain the plan is properly funded.

PEOs that offer self-funded plans will purchase stop-loss coverage from a major insurance carrier, which allows the plan's participants to access that carrier's network of service providers. In most cases, that same carrier will serve as the third-party administrator (TPA) by managing claims. Functioning as both the reinsurer and

TPA, these carriers provide an insurance card bearing the carrier's logo to the insured. So from the employee's point of view, these self-funded health plans function the exact same way as a fully insured plan, with the major difference being plan flexibility and how claims are funded.

But what if the PEO is not big enough to self-insure or even to qualify for a master health plan? As I stated back in chapter one, there are over nine hundred PEOs in this country, and most of them are boutique shops with fewer than two thousand worksite employees. So it stands to reason that most PEOs are simply not large enough to self-fund or to sponsor a master health plan with a major carrier. For example, a PEO with two thousand worksite employees is most likely only going to have 15–20 percent participation in a health plan, and that's just not big enough to have a national plan of its own. In those cases, PEOs who are also licensed brokers will source individual client-based policies and provide their clients with the options that best match their employees' needs. So even PEOs without a master health plan can provide tremendous value to their clients. PEOs study and shop the markets and are experts at understanding complex plan designs in the context of premium cost. Most importantly, PEOs help their clients sort through all the malaise that is health insurance, to maximize the value of their healthcare spending.

So when a small-business owner is evaluating which PEO is right for their business, even though a competitive group health-insurance plan may be a driving factor, cost alone shouldn't be the *deciding* factor.

WORKERS' COMPENSATION

Workers' compensation insurance is regulated at the state level, and every employer is required by law to have it. Although there are similarities, state laws can vary on a number of factors, such as the type of injuries that are covered, the value of certain types of injuries and disabilities, and who gets to choose the treating physician, just to name a few. Because the rules vary and can be complex, many employers find outsourcing this risk to PEOs to be an attractive option. Not only does the employer receive the coverage required by law, but they also usually receive it at a deeply discounted premium. And most PEOs can implement valuable safety-training programs that over

Because the rules vary and can be complex, many employers find outsourcing this risk to PEOs to be an attractive option.

time can lower the employer's overall cost. But as I pointed out in chapter four, thorough underwriting and risk placement of new clients is a matter of survival for PEOs that are willing to accept that risk. It is particularly important for those PEOs with master plans to be selective about which clients they allow to participate. PEOs are ever-mindful of their NCCI-experience modifier, often referred to as a MOD. Workers' compensation premiums rise and fall with the MOD. So for a PEO, effective underwriting and claims management is not optional: it is essential. For this reason, most midsize and larger PEOs invest heavily in risk-management personnel and practices.

In addition to their master plan, they may also maintain multiple workers' compensation plans, each with rates and deductibles. The objective is to have options when analyzing a prospective client's risk, because the more options you have, the more deals you are likely to close. For smaller PEOs or those just getting started, plan options may be limited—if they are available at all. Many small PEOs that don't have the stomach for risk may only be able to offer their clients a guaranteed-cost policy with little or no deductible. While there is very little risk in these plans for the PEO or its client, they are among the most expensive plans on the market because the carrier assumes all the risk. These plans are typically arranged in what is called a multiple-coordinated policy (MCP), where the PEO serves as the plan administrator and aggregator but where each client is individually underwritten and has its own policy within the overall structure. The PEO serves as a kind of "umbrella," a central point for billing, policy administration, and claims reporting. One of the advantages to this type of arrangement is that the client company's experience is maintained and reported individually, meaning that one bad operator will not impact the cost of other companies in the MCP.

As is the case with health insurance, workers' compensation plans can be fully insured or self-funded, and the client seldom knows the difference. Self-funded is where the big boys play. PEOs that have perfected the practice of underwriting and risk management may choose to self-fund a high-deductible plan. Why? Because if they are good at it, workers' compensation can be a profit center for the PEO. A PEO with effective underwriting and safety best practices can qualify for a master plan with a large deductible in exchange for a deeply discounted rate. The PEO will be required to provide collateral adequate to cover the carrier's exposure for the deductible amount. For example, a PEO may choose to take on a deductible of $1 million in exchange for an 80 percent discount on premiums. Since most claims occur under this deductible level, the carrier agrees to the rate so long as the PEO provides a letter of credit or other collateral acceptable to the carrier.

If the standard premium in a guaranteed-cost plan for a particular class code were $3.00 per $100.00 in payroll, the PEO would pay the carrier a premium of $0.60 per $100.00. The PEO may then offer coverage to the client at a discount of 20 percent off the standard rate, or $2.40 per $100.00. In this simplified example, the PEO would then have $1.80 per $100.00 to pay claims ($2.40–$0.60), and to the extent that the PEO can successfully implement risk-management strategies that result in controlling claims to something less than $1.80, the PEO makes a profit. But the reverse is also true. If claims exceed $1.80, the PEO absorbs the loss.

INDUSTRY EXPERIENCE

Although all PEOs deliver the same set of services to their clients, most PEOs have certain industries in which they have more experience than others. From trucking to assisted living to medical practices, different industries can have specific regulations that a PEO should be familiar with for it to effectively help manage its clients' HR. And although it is rare, some PEOs actually *specialize* in particular industries.

So when a small dental practice is shopping around for a PEO and finds one that has a great benefits package but virtually no medical clients, that dental practice would be wise to keep searching. At Lyons HR, we serve a wide range of industries. If we get a call from a charter school, we can offer it at least four references of other charter schools we work with. Or if a physician calls and wants to know our experience with the medical industry, we can offer her a list of references to help her make an informed and confident decision.

The bottom line is this: despite all the drivers that compel a small business to pursue a relationship with a PEO, finding one with relevant industry experience and a list of references should be among the top qualifiers.

CERTIFICATION AND ACCREDITATION

As we've seen, there are number of factors that a small business should consider when trying to determine which PEO is right for it. In chapter five, we explored the Small Business Efficiency Act and the long-awaited federal legal certainty it ushered in for the industry. Along with this legal certainty, the SBEA created the voluntary IRS-certification program, which for many is now the minimum standard used to measure a PEO's fiscal responsibility. I need to emphasize the word *voluntary* here, because not all PEOs choose to participate in the program. The rigorous application process and the expenses of ongoing reporting and bonding requirements are thought to be too burdensome for some PEO operators. But for those of us who do participate, we believe the value and protections that certification provides to our clients outweighs the costs. In addition to eliminating wage-base restarts and preserving all federal tax credits for our clients, as a certified PEO (CPEO), we assume *sole* liability for the collection and remission of all federal payroll taxes. It is true that all PEOs take on the responsibility of remitting the federal payroll taxes of their clients. But if the PEO is not certified, the client can still be held liable by the IRS for those taxes if the PEO defaults on payment. Clients of CPEOs can be assured that they will never be held liable, because once they have remitted taxes to the PEO, the situation is treated the same as if their taxes had been remitted directly to the IRS. This fact provides added peace of mind for the client.

But federal payroll taxes are only one employer liability. What about all the other employer liabilities, like state withholdings, benefits deductions, and garnishments? What assurance can a PEO client have that all these employer liabilities will be satisfied? The answer is accreditation by the Employer Services Assurance Corporation (ESAC).

Established in 1995 by NAPEO, ESAC is an independent nonprofit corporation and is the official accreditation and financial-assurance organization for the PEO industry. Accreditation provides PEO clients with assurances for not only federal payroll-tax compliance but also for the full range of employer liabilities, and that performance is backed by millions of dollars in surety bonds held in trust. In fact, ESAC accreditation is so comprehensive that many states accept it in lieu of some or all of their own PEO-licensing requirements.

To be accredited by ESAC, a PEO must meet and maintain certain ethical, financial, and operational standards established by ESAC's board of directors. And maintaining this accreditation requires the PEO to submit quarterly attestations to ESAC in compliance with audited, agreed-upon procedures conducted by an independent CPA. The ESAC accreditation standards are updated periodically by its board of directors, which is made up of former state and federal regulators and experienced PEO operators, as well as industry attorneys and CPAs, who collectively have well over a hundred years of experience in the industry. Earning accreditation demonstrates a PEO's financial stability, ethical business conduct, and adherence to operational standards and regulatory requirements.

ESAC's stated mission is to build integrity and trust and to provide assurance to the PEO industry, so that the industry can reach its full potential in support of America's small businesses. ESAC accreditation has long been considered the gold standard for PEO best practices and financial reliability. But because the standards are so high, fewer than 5 percent of PEOs have earned this distinction. Applicants are subject to extensive background checks on all controlling persons within the PEO to verify their professional experience and competence over a full range of business disciplines. Background checks must also verify a history of complying with all state and federal laws. In addition to these ethical standards, there are twenty-one financial standards that must be met and maintained. The maintaining of liquidity ratios and the establishing of minimum net worth, net working capital, and reserve requirements for loss-sensitive insurance plans are among those financial standards. Finally, there are eighteen operational standards which focus primarily on policy, procedure, and internal control. In all, there are forty-four standards that must be initially met, then maintained for a PEO to be accredited. And they are all crafted with the purpose of protecting the client by ensuring the solvency of the PEO.

In fact, since the program was established in 1995, there has never been a default by an accredited PEO.

But are there any alternatives to PEOs in terms of providing HR services to clients? The answer is *yes*, there are certainly alternatives, though none as complete or comprehensive in serving all of a client's HR needs. Let's draw some comparisons with two of the more well-known alternatives to PEOs: ASOs and SaaS.

PEOS VERSUS ASOS

Administrative Service Organizations, or ASOs, provide outsourced HR and administrative services such as payroll for their clients, very much like the services provided by a PEO. The major difference between an ASO and a PEO is, in a single word, *coemployment*. In the ASO relationship, the client outsources administrative tasks but retains all the employment-related risks and liabilities, and the client remains the employer of record for tax purposes. Taxes and insurance filings may be managed by the ASO, but they are filed under the client's federal identification number, not the ASO's. In a PEO relationship, the PEO must be an employer for the employees to be able to take advantage of the PEO's workers' compensation and benefit plans, and it's the only way the client can benefit from shared employer liability. In a coemployer relationship, the client is always the common-law employer, and the PEO is the statutory employer, but in an ASO relationship, there is no coemployment. An ASO could be providing many of the same services that a PEO is providing, but the ASO is not the statutory employer. An ASO simply provides administrative services to its clients, denying those small businesses any economy-of-scale benefits typically associated with a PEO.

The term *ASO* was actually coined by the PEO industry in the late 1990s, because there was so much confusion around this subject. It was important for the industry to distinguish between the full-scale comprehensive services offered by PEOs and the a-la-carte HR-support services offered by these administrative-support firms. So why would a business choose ASO over PEO? Before the passage of the SBEA, many PEOs used the ASO model as a temporary bridge to onboard new clients and to avoid payroll-tax wage-base restarts. Sometimes, larger companies who have their own HR infrastructure may be looking to outsource only their payroll or benefits administration, and an ASO could be a good option for them. Most clients who choose the ASO option tend to have more employees. There are also government municipalities and nonprofit organizations that need managed services but are prohibited from using a PEO because of the coemployment designation. So because there are some instances when the ASO model makes more sense, most PEOs offer both services.

PEOS VERSUS SAAS

There has been a deluge of new cloud-based HR-software products that have been launched over the past few years, each one promoting that its product has "everything you need," including payroll, time, talent, and HR. Radio ads make these sound great, and they have attracted some real attention in the marketplace. After all, millennials are the largest demographic in today's workforce, and they are comfortable with self-service technology. All these online HR platforms are referred to as SaaS, which is an acronym for "Software as a Service."

SaaS is an HR-management platform that is, for the most part, self-service. Many of these SaaS platforms offer impressive technology with intuitive workflows and reporting capabilities. Because these have gained popularity in recent years, some PEOs have developed SaaS platforms as a secondary line of business. A simple Google search will bring up the names of dozens of options, and from there, a company can schedule an online demo before purchasing a subscription. But what happens when the client has a problem and needs professional guidance?

Think about the difference between QuickBooks software and having a CPA on call. The software alternative is certainly convenient, and if you understand accounting and know what you are doing, you can use it to maintain your general ledger and to generate financial statements and other useful management reports. But what if you are not an accountant, and your general ledger doesn't balance, or what if you have a tax question? You can spend the time to resolve it yourself, or you can call your CPA for help. With a PEO service, you not only get robust HR technology, but you also get a team of experts whom you can email or call for any and all HR-related issues. Think about the Pillars of Profitability we talked about earlier. SaaS doesn't provide that kind of real-time, human subject-matter expertise. Small businesses opting for SaaS are basically leasing space on the software company's platform, then having to do everything themselves. And since they are only leasing software, there is no risk mitigation or employment-liability sharing with SaaS. That only happens with the PEO-coemployment model.

Most SaaS platforms have a human-resource information system (HRIS) database, where all of the employee documentation, notes, anniversaries, and training credentials, among other things, are stored. They have a payroll component, much like QuickBooks, where employees' compensation is tracked and distributed using the software. But there is a significant lack of customization available. PEOs, by contrast, can create specific HR-service plans based on the needs of each client by leveraging technology. PEOs make everything accessible to their clients with just one login through a single online portal; but more importantly, there is an actual subject-matter expert on the other end of the line, who knows your business and is there to help you. PEOs use technology as a tool to deliver professional services, but the technology is not itself the service. As those of us in the industry often say, "you can't spell people without PEO!"

Both ASOs and SaaS have their functions, but there isn't a software or administration service out there that can compare to the cost savings and expert help a relationship with a PEO provides.

At the end of the day, PEOs exist to make small businesses more profitable and to help them be more efficient. Dan McHenry, arguably the most-recognized authority and most-sought-after con-sultant to the PEO industry, always says that the purpose of a PEO is to do three things for its clients: Help them make more money; help them keep more of what they make; and protect their assets.

Everything that the PEO does for small businesses can be tied to those three objectives.

CHAPTER SEVEN

CULTURE CREATORS

The beatings will continue until morale improves.

—Unknown Origin

J oe pulled into his parking lot on a typical Friday morning and couldn't ignore the eerie feeling in his stomach. Something just seemed odd. The shop appeared to be abandoned, and it was well after 8:00 a.m.

Where is everyone? he thought. *Is today a holiday that I just forgot about?*

Joe checked his watch and wondered what was going on. As he approached the front door to the shop, he noticed there were no lights on inside.

"Something is definitely wrong," he said to himself.

Joe opened the front door and heard the word "Surprise!" shouted in unison by all his employees. After all, twenty-five years in business is quite an accomplishment.

Chandler had been planning a surprise anniversary celebration for weeks. He coordinated the schedules of Joe's other shops to be certain all twenty-five employees could be on hand for the big celebration. Chandler had been with Joe since the very beginning and was now running day-to-day operations. Chandler thought back to when he was still in high school, when Joe gave him a chance. It was just him, Joe, and Judy trying to build an auto-repair business from scratch. They had all put in some long hours. Joe and Chandler had toiled away under the hood while Judy had struggled to keep all the bills paid. As Chandler watched the festivities unfold, he felt a profound sense of appreciation for all that Joe had done for him.

Thanks to the guidance from his PEO, Joe's corporate culture is a far cry from this chapter's opening quote. That simple phrase from a bygone era is amusing in its irony, but its sentiment reflects some of the more-draconian management styles from the past. Instead, Joe has created and maintained a corporate culture that pays out the invaluable dividends of employee respect, appreciation, and job satisfaction—which in turn directly influences the success of Joe's business.

For better or worse, every organization has a culture. It will either be one that evolves on its own or one that is purposeful and strategically developed over time. If you're fortunate enough to work with an organization that has a strong and positive corporate culture, you'll probably know it. Unfortunately, if the culture is toxic, you'll know that, too.

The very concept of culture isn't unique to business, as you well know. In fact, the corporate world borrowed the word *culture* from sociologists, who use the term when referring to a particular set of beliefs and behaviors specific to a region of the world. We have Asian culture, European culture, American culture—and drilling even deeper into the latter, we can subdivide into Southern culture, New England culture, and West Coast culture, among dozens of others.

No matter the context, culture informs behaviors and attitudes of the people within it. When it comes to an organization's culture, it's not just about overall morale. And it's certainly not just about compensation or benefits either. Instead, a company's culture comes down to intangible qualities of character.

When someone has eyes on them, they are more likely to be on their best behavior. But the essence of *who* a person is—that is revealed when they're by themselves.

In much the same way, a business has an intangible asset called culture, essentially the character of a company. It's either a positive influence on a business's performance, or it's a drag on it. And it's completely up to the leadership of a business whether or not it allows the culture to evolve on its own or makes it a strategic initiative. If the leadership makes culture a strategic initiative, then it has to determine which behaviors to reward and encourage. What are the behaviors that will enhance the customers' experiences? Once the leadership answers that question, it will have to create goals about those types of behaviors. With a PEO at its back, a small business's leadership can create the culture of success it's always dreamed of.

Of course, this is assuming that a business owner does all of the core things right and delivers a valuable product or service at a competitive price. But outside of that, a good culture is the single-most-important factor that can really launch a company into orbit. This underscores the point that as important as a business's customers are, the *employees* are actually more critical to the business. Think about it: they are the ones who are interacting with customers on a day-in, day-out basis. If employees have a good attitude, that comes through in their interaction with the customers. If they have a sour attitude, that also comes through. Culture is the filter through which those employee–customer interactions occur. And as each customer is unique, so is every single employee.

> A dynamic corporate culture is one that leverages its diversity to drive exceptional employee performance, recognizing the uniqueness of the individual while also promoting common goals and a shared purpose.

In fact, today's workforce is a virtual melting pot of five different generations, all with distinctive work styles that must be accommodated in the workplace. A dynamic corporate culture is one that leverages its diversity to drive exceptional employee performance, recognizing the uniqueness of the individual while also promoting common goals and a shared purpose.

GENERATIONS OF CULTURES

We have in some companies five different generations of people working together today. The Silent Generation, born before World War II, are those who are defined by a strong work ethic, who have a sense of loyalty and discipline, and who are very value driven. Then we have the Baby Boomers who bridge the gap between the older traditionalist approach to business and the newer technology-driven economy that we have today.

Next, of course, are the Gen-Xers. Raised by the Boomers, they grew into a generation of independent, resourceful, and self-sufficient individuals, who inherently dislike being micromanaged and who embrace a hands-off management philosophy. The Millennial generation is next and already represents the majority of the modern workforce. These people are tech-savvy and driven; they have high expectations of their employers, and they aren't afraid to question authority. Millennials also tend to value the work experience over other factors, such as compensation. This characteristic also rings true for our youngest generation, the iGen. As the name implies, these folks are out-of-the-box thinkers, mobile-device driven, and extremely creative.

People in marketing know these generational characteristics well and market their products accordingly, in an effort to cover the entire spectrum. They study the attitudes and behaviors, the wants and needs of the various demographics, because they know that if they can tap into that, they can connect with the consumer. The same can be said for the employer in the workplace. By understanding the psychology of the generations of employees, a business owner can work to create a culture where common values, ideals, goals, and ethics intersect.

A strong culture is one of pride and teamwork that encourages everyone to reach their full potential. It supports and celebrates the success of others and affirms personal accountability. It empowers people by promoting professional development and recognizes the value that a skilled and motivated workforce delivers. A strong culture is one where everyone is treated with fairness and respect, where a healthy balance between work and family is promoted, and where employees love their jobs and are committed to the success of the organization. A strong culture rewards those who demonstrate their commitment through initiative, passion, and a willingness to do more than is expected. A strong culture is measured by employee and customer loyalty.

Cultivating a strong culture begins by clearly defining the organization's vision and mission and by establishing a solid set of uncompromising company values that everybody can get behind, no matter which generation they represent. To illustrate what I mean, I would like to share our company values—what we at Lyons HR believe to be the cornerstone of our culture.

MISSION STATEMENT

Our mission is to improve the lives of our clients, employees, and coworkers by implementing smarter workforce-management strategies.

Establishing the right set of values and then living by them is the single biggest factor in developing the culture you want. It's not only important that values be properly identified, but they must also be routinely communicated throughout the organization. Everyone should know what they are, because a company's value system will dictate how its people will react to any situation. Values define who you are as an organization, or if you are in development, whom you want to become. Because we are in the people business, PEOs understand the impact a healthy culture has on productivity perhaps more acutely than those outside our industry. We are, after all, people serving other people, and a PEO with a healthy culture can have a huge influence on the culture of its clients. PEOs encourage their clients to develop culture keystones, and PEOs can be instrumental in helping them maintain that culture to help them achieve their corporate goals.

Many years ago, we established ten values that would define who we are. I want to share these with you and explain why they are an intricate part of everything we do.

SERVICE

How can a company that provides professional services not have "Service" as one of its core values? We exist to serve not only our customers but also each other! Achieving service excellence while continuously striving for perfection is our goal. So often we hear companies make the bold claim that their customer service is the best in the business. But how do you know that for sure? Do you have an effective Customer Relationship Management (CRM) system that measures service delivery? Do you receive positive client feedback through surveys and testimonials? And how do you know you are effectively serving your teammates? Are you asking for honest feedback from those you work with or supervise?

There are two essential keys to building a strong service organization. The first is in hiring the right attitude, and the second is in effective training. I have always believed when hiring that attitude trumps skills. In my experience I have learned you can always train good people to perform tasks, but you can't always change an attitude that's not already preconditioned for service.

TEAMWORK

Building strong teams is a process that takes time. Like a professional sports organization, the best teams are made up of members who each possess a unique set of skills that make the team stronger as a whole. The PEO business model is complex and requires expertise in a wide range of subjects. So when PEOs refer to their services as being provided by "a team of subject-matter experts," that's *literally* what they mean. Our safety-and-risk professionals bring a different set of skills than our legal team brings. And our tax team offers a different value than our technology or benefits groups. Each skill is valuable and important on its own, but when there is shared vision by those subject-matter experts, those different skills can be coordinated in a way that generates a much higher value.

INTEGRITY

Doing what is right, honest, and honorable in all things, regardless of the consequences: that's how we define integrity at Lyons HR. And it's an integral part of everything we do. It's always doing what's in the best interest of our clients, even if that means we lose their business. Over the past twenty-five years, there have been times when we were asked to "look the other way" on matters involving ethics or fair dealing, and in every case, doing what is right and honorable has been our guiding principle. Integrity is being completely transparent, acknowledging your mistakes, and doing everything humanly possible to correct them. It's about always telling the truth in any situation, because there is no such thing as degrees of integrity. You either have it, or you don't.

RESPECT

Have you ever been talked down to? If you are like most everyone I know, you probably have, and you know how terrible it made you feel. The quickest way I know to create a toxic culture is to allow an elitist class of people to develop the idea that "my job is more important than your job" or that "this company couldn't survive without me." If you spot that attitude, you had better purge it from the organization before it takes root and infects your culture. Simply put, there is no place in any organization for condescension of any kind. Even constructive criticism, which is sometimes needed, can be delivered in a way that is respectful.

Disagreements can be a good thing if there is mutual respect. Different opinions should be welcomed and debated respectfully, and ideas that on the surface may seem a bit wacky should be encouraged. Why? Because the best ideas and innovations come from people who are not afraid to fail and who are encouraged to freely express their opinions.

ACCOUNTABILITY

The PEO business can be characterized by a series of hard deadlines, and when you have multiple departments, and one department cannot proceed until the preceding department completes its tasks, accountability is the lubrication that keeps things moving. If done right, accountability isn't something that needs much supervision. In fact, with a good culture, it's self-imposed. Employees have their own internal barometer that tells them when they are holding up their coworkers or if an oversight on their end has clogged the system.

EXCELLENCE

Excellence is a standard that is never compromised. In other words, it actually *sets* the standard. But keep in mind that excellence is not the same thing as perfection, because perfection is impossible. Excellence means never compromising and constantly striving to improve. Imagine excellence like an escalator. As it's going down, you're at the bottom of that escalator trying to walk up. If you take steps at the same pace the escalator is moving, what happens? You end up in the same place. But if you can set a faster pace than what is coming at you, you set a stride that will eventually take you to the top.

EMPOWERMENT

Empowerment is directly related to confidence. When an employee feels empowered, they will be confident in their decisions and their interactions with clients. At Lyons HR we encourage our people to continually expand their knowledge and to expand themselves professionally. We want them to feel free to take calculated risks and to think outside the box. Because we don't expect perfection, our employees have the autonomy and confidence to accomplish their corporate goals in new and exciting ways. And at the end of the day, they know we have their backs.

A healthy culture allows employees to experiment, to expand, and to dream.

ADAPTIVITY

Perhaps there has never been a value that is timelier than this one. Businesses all over the world are being forced to adapt to new conditions brought on by the COVID-19 pandemic. But in business, there is *forced adaptation*, and then there is *chosen adaptation*. In the case of COVID-19, the government required businesses to adapt to new safety protocols as a condition of reopening. Restaurants and bars come to mind, but those changes are about as subtle as being smacked in the face with a shovel. Here, I'm talking about recognizing the need to adapt when doing so is less obvious. In business, you have three options: you create innovation; you are an adapter of innovation; or you are destroyed by innovation. All adults today remember a company called Blockbuster Video, which ignored a start-up service called Netflix, and we all know how that turned out. Because the world changes so quickly, if your business is not able to recognize trends and adapt to change, it will never survive.

RELATIONSHIPS

The PEO business is a relationship business. We've talked about the value of teamwork as it relates to internal relationships with our colleagues. But a strong culture is one that also seeks and embraces external strategic partnerships that are mutually rewarding. We believe in nurturing vendor relationships just as much as we do client relationships. Like everyone else, we want the best deal we can get, but we also want our vendor partners to make money on us so they will continue to provide the services we depend on. We realize they can't do that if the return is not there.

By the same token, we appreciate it when our clients tell us that we provide far more value than we cost. At Lyons HR, we call those "Raving Fan Awards," and any time one of our teammates gets one from a client, we share it within the company. A healthy culture is one that celebrates successes and also shares failures together. If a vendor or client relationship is all one-sided, it's never going to work. If one side does all the giving and the other side does all the taking, that's going to run its course, eventually. So the key to developing long-term strategic relationships is to find that delicate place where both parties are receiving a higher value from the relationship than it costs. When that balance tilts too heavily to one side, it won't be long until one party will be forced to call it quits.

FUN

This one is my favorite. I say to my employees all the time, "I want this to be the best job you've ever had." Of course, having fun and enjoying your work doesn't mean you don't get serious and get things done. But any time and every time we have an opportunity to come together for good, healthy social interaction—where we're getting to know each other on a personal level; we're getting to know each other's family dynamics; and we're getting to know their hobbies and passions—the culture becomes that much stronger.

Because we operate from different campuses, it is not always easy to stay connected, and annual picnics and holiday parties are just not enough to promote the culture we want. So we make it a priority to schedule something fun at least once a month. Our company newsletter always includes a write-up of the fun event from the prior month, complete with pictures of our teams engaged in funny, sometimes even goofy, social interaction. For example, each year at Halloween we encourage our team members to wear costumes to the office. Not everyone participates, but most do. And we actually have a contest and award prizes for the most-creative costume. A couple of years ago, I came to the office dressed as Elvis, complete with the white-sequined jumpsuit, black wig and sideburns, and gaudy, oversized sunglasses. Frankly, I looked ridiculous, but it generated a lot of laughs, and it gave our people an opportunity to see me in a completely different light.

When you can walk through the halls of a business and hear people laughing, sharing personal stories that happened in their lives, celebrating their team members, or supporting each other in times of sorrow, that's when you know you've created something much greater than a work environment—a family of sorts. That is the essence of culture.

CULTURE IN ACTION

Culture is so important to Lyons HR and to me personally that we actually have a person on our payroll dedicated to it—our "coordinator of people and culture." We also created something we call our Partner's Council, which is made up of representatives from various departments. Our culture coordinator facilitates quarterly agenda-driven meetings with the Partner's Council, so that our leadership can gather unfiltered feedback from the ground troops. We want to know what would make their jobs better, what would make them more efficient at their jobs, and what would make them enjoy their jobs more.

Of course, we want to know what we're doing well, but we also want constructive feedback. For example, we recently moved our primary operations center in Gadsden, Alabama, from an office building of about 8,500 square feet into a newly remodeled nineteen-thousand-square-foot office building. You can imagine with over fifty people working from that first location, we were constantly receiving feedback that we simply needed more space—and that the restroom facilities were not adequate for that number of people and that we needed a larger break room.

So when we bought the new building, we didn't just turn a very large space in the back into a breakroom: we turned it into a 1950s-style diner, complete with pictures of Elvis, The Rat Pack, Marilyn Monroe, and classic cars. We even have booth-style seating. In fact, it looks so much like a real diner that we once had someone come in through the rear entrance, sit down, and attempt to order lunch!

PEOs are in a unique position to positively impact their clients' company cultures—first, in leading by example. PEOs become highly engaged with their clients and, more importantly, with their clients' employees. PEOs don't just prepare payroll and administer benefits; they are experts at crafting HR policy and conducting effective employee-training and professional-development programs that are fun and innovative and that promote the kind of culture that leads to higher employee engagement and performance. PEOs help their clients take care of their people. After all, happy employees make happy clients. Happy clients make loyal clients. And loyal clients make profitable companies.

Employees want more than a job; they want a sense of purpose, and a good PEO helps its clients achieve this for their employees. Employees want to know that there's opportunity to grow within the organization; they want to feel and to share in the successes of the company and to understand their contribution to that success; they want to feel appreciated and respected by their coworkers; and they want to have confidence in their leadership.

These are the things that drive a culture to greatness.

CHAPTER EIGHT

CRISIS MANAGEMENT

It's not the strongest of the species that survives, nor the most intelligent ... It is the one that is most adaptable to change.

—Charles Darwin

I n the five years since Joe signed on with his PEO partner, he has focused on expanding his existing shops, setting up a new repair shop, and hiring and training new mechanics. In that short period of time, he developed three locations into fully mature profit centers that seem to always be busy with repair work. Joe has always wanted to be more involved in his local community, but never seemed to have the time. Now, he is serving on his local chamber board and has also started playing golf twice a week with a group of friends. Joe's PEO has practically eliminated the time Joe and Judy used to spend on employee issues, and as a result, business profits have almost doubled over the past five years.

But just when his circumstances couldn't get much better, Joe, just like the rest of the world, was about to be shaken to his core. As the old saying goes, you can't always control what happens to you, but you can control how you react to it … and Joe was about to be tested like never before.

As the COVID-19 pandemic began to surge in the United States, small-business owners like Joe found themselves dealing with a problem that had no precedent. There was no playbook to provide guidance on how to manage a business through a pandemic. Not like this one!

In a matter of just a few weeks, Joe found the repair work at his shops was off by over 50 percent. Even though auto-repair shops were designated an essential business by the government, with most people sheltering at home, there just wasn't as much work to be done.

What a quandary, Joe thought to himself. *I've spent the past twenty-five years growing this business and building a reputation. I've trained over fifty aspiring technicians and finally have a well-trained staff and processes in place to run things in my absence. I finally have this business where I want it. And now, without any warning, I stand to lose it all!*

With twenty-five employees on payroll and no new work coming in, Joe has a decision to make.

Should I lay off some of my employees until this thing passes, or should I just ride it out?

Joe knows he can't afford to keep everyone, with the work drying up. And he has no way of knowing when business will return to normal, if ever. If he furloughs his technicians, he might not be able to get them back when he needs them. And if he keeps them on payroll, he may go broke.

Joe watches the nightly news, trying to make sense of all the talking heads arguing back and forth. But he is left confused by all the bickering. Fortunately, Joe's PEO has been monitoring developments at both the state and federal level and is updating Joe daily with breaking news. It is Joe's PEO that advises him regarding the CARES Act and guides him through the loan application process. It is Joe's PEO that provides the data needed to complete his loan application under the SBA's Payroll Protection Program. And as Joe's business begins to gradually recover and restrictions are eased, it is Joe's PEO that provides a safe return-to-work policy and crafts reopening protocols based on public-safety guidelines. As Joe depletes the PPP loan proceeds, it is his PEO that provides the data and again assists when it comes time to apply for and maximize his loan forgiveness. Joe's business dropped off dramatically over the course of the pandemic, but because of the PPP loan, his employees never missed a day of work and never missed a paycheck.

The effects of COVID-19 on small businesses, even those that survived the economic shutdown, will continue to resonate for years, if not decades, to come. But as frightening and overwhelming as a crisis can be, it is hardly unique. Granted, some may be worse than others, and certain crises affect some small businesses without impacting others at all.

Yet as we saw with this chapter's opening story about Joe, of all the value propositions a PEO brings to the table for the small-business owner, probably the biggest advantage PEO clients receive is that skilled, knowledgeable, level-headed team of experts in their corner to manage a crisis when it hits. And trust me, large or small, crises hit more often than you may realize …

THE CRISIS CYCLE

Lyons HR is headquartered in northern Alabama—prime tornado territory. Each season, there's always a risk of tornadoes wreaking havoc on the homes and businesses in our area. Other coastal states in the southeastern United States need to be prepared for hurricane season every year. Small-business owners in states like California need to have a plan of action in place in case of a wildfire or even a devastating earthquake. And small businesses in the northern Midwest and New England states must deal with the looming threat of crippling blizzards each winter.

Natural disasters can cause critical infrastructure crashes, disrupted operations, building damage, and human casualties. Yet these crises are understood as inevitable, to varying degrees, by the locals who have their businesses in these areas. Disaster-recovery plans and crisis management are just part of the equation of running a business, or at least they should be. And in case you're wondering, yes, PEOs routinely assist clients with putting those plans in place for a worst-case scenario.

But about every decade or so, it seems, the world goes through a massive upheaval in normal operations. The Gulf War of the early 1990s. The uncertainty of Y2K. The terrorist attacks on US soil on September 11, 2001. The Great Recession and housing crisis of the late 2000s. And now COVID-19 in 2020.

It is during these unexpected events that our sense of normalcy and security, our dreams for the future, and even our character are challenged. These times present a special challenge to small-business owners because each of these events disrupted the economy and ushered in sweeping regulatory changes in the workplace. With PEOs by their sides however, small-business owners can feel a sense of business continuity that safeguards their most important assets: their people.

When you think of all the forms a crisis can take; from financial scandal to natural disasters, from cyberattacks to violence in the workplace, the COVID-19 crisis is unique in one very important way. It has, to some degree, affected virtually every person in the world. It has presented challenges not just for a few US industries, but *all* industries worldwide, even those that saw a massive demand increase like Amazon.

THE COVID-19 CRISIS

The date was January 28, 2020 when I heard the word *coronavirus* for the first time. I remember not paying that much attention to it, because the real threat posed by the pandemic was not yet general knowledge. But within just a few weeks, the Coronavirus Disease 2019, or COVID-19 (as it was named on February 11 by the World Health Organization) was the story dominating every news cycle. New cases were being confirmed across the globe, and despite early travel bans imposed by the Trump administration, the pandemic reached the United States, with the first confirmed case in Washington state in late January.

To say that small-business owners were not prepared for COVID-19 is a monumental understatement. The year 2019 had ended strongly with the stock market at a record high, while unemployment was at a fifty-year low. Small business in the United States was thriving, but in a matter of just a few weeks, small-business owners went from record profits to struggling for their very survival. The pandemic was threatening our lives, our economy, and our way of life. On March 13, the Trump administration declared a national emergency, and by March 26, the United States led the world in new confirmed cases and deaths. By March 30, stay-at-home orders were being mandated across the country in a desperate effort to slow the spread of the pandemic. So with the economy effectively shut down for an undetermined period of time, small-business owners across the country wondered how they would survive.

The first action taken by Congress in response to the pandemic was the Families First Coronavirus Response Act (FFCRA). In a rare show of bipartisanship, Congress passed the legislation on March 18, and it was quickly signed by President Trump. Outside providing a tax credit to offset the cost of employee leave associated with COVID-19, the FFCRA did little to help small businesses. The FFCRA was designed primarily to help employees who were either infected or who were caring for an infected family member, by providing paid sick leave and by expanding leave provisions under the FMLA. It was the Coronavirus Aid, Relief, and Economic Security (CARES) Act, which passed less than two weeks later, that provided relief specifically targeting business owners. The $2.2 trillion CARES Act, administered by the Small Business Administration, created several programs for small businesses, including debt relief under the Small Business Debt Program and the Economic Injury Disaster Loan program (EIDL). But by far, the most popular program created by the CARES Act was the Payroll Protection Program (PPP Loans) which was designed to help businesses keep employees on their payroll during the pandemic. Qualifying businesses could borrow up to two-and-a-half times their average monthly payroll costs, and the most appealing part of the program was this: so long as the borrower used the loan proceeds for payroll costs, rent, utilities, or mortgage interest, it could all be forgiven, making the loan essentially a grant.

The CARES Act initially appropriated $350 billion for loans to small businesses with fewer than five hundred employees. But that initial appropriation was soon exhausted, leaving many loan applications unfunded. The resulting public outcry forced Congress to pass a second stimulus that added another $310 billion. As of this writing, Congress is debating additional stimulus bills to help the country combat the pandemic. Although the PPP loan program added significantly to the national debt, it was the lifeline small-business owners needed to hopefully get through the crisis. And as expected, when the program passed, banks were overwhelmed by PPP loan applications.

Small-business owners around the country had shifted into survival mode well before the CARES Act passed. Many states had already issued mandatory closures of certain nonessential businesses like restaurants, bars, fitness gyms, and salons, and many of these businesses had no choice but to furlough employees until they were able to reopen, if at all. To complicate matters further, the nonstop twenty-four-hour news cycle, along with all the new legislation coming out of Washington, left many business owners confused and struggling to decide the best path forward. There was just too much information coming at them all at once.

The CARES Act had several well-intentioned provisions, but because it was passed so quickly, it produced some unintended consequences. For example, the CARES Act created the Federal Pandemic Unemployment Compensation (FPUC) program, which provided federal funding for furloughed employees each to receive an additional $600 per week in unemployment compensation through the end of July, in addition to the amount they could collect under state law. This was a noble gesture on the part of Congress, but the result was, in many cases, that employees could earn more being furloughed and collecting unemployment than they could by continuing to work—which was certainly not the intent of the program. Although the DOL issued guidance that benefits paid under the FPUC program would not be charged against employers' unemployment-claims experience, many employers still had difficulty persuading furloughed employees to return to work.

Since the FFCRA passed on March 18, there was a continuous release of new regulations issued by the SBA and the Treasury Department related to COVID-19, and PEOs have been on the front lines monitoring these developments in real time, so they could advise their clients. This important legislation was not a one-size-fits-all application. When you think of all the unique circumstances a business can have, perhaps the biggest advantage clients of PEOs have received during this time is having a partner who is interpreting the rapidly changing legislation hourly, to ensure they are kept informed and remain compliant.

Conditions on the ground were changing by the hour, and we knew our clients would have a wide range of questions. But this was uncharted territory, with brand new legislation and regulatory updates happening almost daily. How could we respond to our clients' questions when these programs were so new and there was no clear guidance? This is where I get to brag on our industry association, NAPEO. It did an outstanding job of keeping the industry informed, and that enabled PEOs across the country to pass vital information to their clients during this time of rapid change. For example, NAPEO staff monitored legislative developments around the clock, then conducted webinars within twenty-four hours free of charge to all their members. NAPEO provided easy-to-understand summaries, including interpretation of the SBA's FAQs about the popular PPP loan program. It would then post these webinars on its website for later viewing. It was this critical support early on from

NAPEO that kept the payroll, HR, tax, and legal teams at Lyons HR up to date on the latest developments.

Even before the CARES Act was enacted, our HR, tax, and payroll teams were preparing for the PPP loan documentation requests that were sure to come our way. During those first few days, we provided hundreds of businesses with the payroll data needed to complete their PPP loan applications, along with an Excel template demonstrating how the loan amount should be calculated. We knew that being ready on day one to respond would make the difference for many in survival or closing shop.

The FFCRA and the CARES Act were passed through Congress at a speed that I have never witnessed in my lifetime. PPP loans were a literal lifeline to millions of small businesses around the country, but they also came with some new payroll-reporting requirements. For the loan to be ultimately forgiven, 75 percent of the loan proceeds had to be used on qualifying payroll costs. Although this percentage was later amended to 60%, it made tracking all payroll costs critically important.

Our clients also had questions about the complexity of furloughed employees being rehired. Did the hire date start over, or should the original hire date be recognized? The answer to that question affected an employee's eligibility for benefits. What if furloughed employees were on COBRA or were collecting unemployment and did not want to return to work? How should that be handled? What about the tax credits available through the FFCRA? Do we qualify for that? How do we track payroll for employees who were on paid extended FMLA? Can I borrow against my 401(k) without penalty? Are furloughed employees' wages still subject to workers' compensation premiums? These are the type of questions our clients were asking, and each question came with that client's unique set of circumstances, making the application of the regulations much more of a challenge. In many instances, clarifying guidance which would have helped answer these questions took weeks to be issued. Still, the questions poured in.

We knew right away that PEO relationships were going to be that critical factor in the difference between closing the doors permanently and riding out the storm for many small businesses. To answer this call to action, we executed the following four key elements necessary in managing any crisis …

A CULTURE OF FIRST RESPONDERS

The true measure of character is found in how someone responds under extreme conditions. Sometimes during times of crisis, people will hide in their bunkers. With the world coming down around them, they try to camouflage themselves and hope that they aren't noticed. And then you have other people who step up and say, "Here I am. Use me. I've got an idea. I've got something that I can bring to the table." That is what I call a culture of first responders—people who don't freeze in fear, but who instead offer to take the reins, to work long hours, and to help their teams and their clients weather the storm. Never was this more on display than during the COVID-19 crisis.

In crisis-management mode, these first responders are calm. They are proficient at removing emotion from the decision-making process, dealing solely with facts, not rumors. And with COVID-19, there were plenty of rumors flying around in the early days. We had people in our company who were naturally worried, wanting to know the outlook of their livelihoods.

As an essential business, Lyons HR was never ordered to close. However, as a preventive strategy and out of concern for our employees and their families, we instituted a company-wide work-from-home policy on March 9. It was imperative that our employees remain safe and that service to our clients continue without interruption. For years, we had operated with a written business-continuity and disaster-recovery plan in anticipation of a natural disaster like a tornado, but this was the first time we had to actually execute on it. We had to spend money on new hardware and equipment—the basic technology needed to get everyone equipped and connected from home. And I must say, I was very proud of the way our team responded.

Due to existing disaster-recovery protocols, the payroll team was able to immediately work from home. And within just a few days, all the members of our entire staff, from all our locations, were working from home. Business continuity is one of the major advantages a small business receives when partnering with a PEO, because most small-business owners are not equipped to withstand a major business disruption. PEOs have the technology and business-continuity plans in place to protect their clients from service disruptions caused by natural disasters, civil unrest, or, as in this case, a pandemic. And as businesses begin to reopen, PEOs are once again there to help craft revised safety protocols based on new federal guidelines.

> **PEOs have the technology and business-continuity plans in place to protect their clients from service disruptions caused by natural disasters, civil unrest, or, as in this case, a pandemic.**

Continuing to deliver services to our clients was a top priority, but it was also important that everyone remain engaged with their teammates, because we believe culture drives productivity. To do this, we created a daily schedule of videoconference meetings using Microsoft Teams, so that we could stay visually connected. Our executive team met twice daily, once at 9:00 a.m. and again at the end of the day at 4:30 p.m. The executive group is made up of our company's president, our CFO, our corporate counsel, our vice presidents, and me. The executives would also meet with their respective teams at scheduled times throughout the day, then give a report to the executive team during our 4:30 p.m. call. I must admit that working through this crisis together has brought us closer as a team than we were before COVID-19, and for that, I am grateful!

ONGOING COMMUNICATION

One of the biggest disruptors when a crisis hits is the sudden change in communication. Both internal and external, as well as in style and substance, the importance of strong, recurring communication cannot be overstated. This fact may seem obvious, but during a crisis, emotions run high, often at the expense of objectivity. And when a crisis hits and routines are suddenly altered, the ability to keep everyone informed and focused on the task at hand is all the more critical. In a crisis, communication must be frequent, and most of all, factual. But COVID-19 changed the way we communicated by forcing a greater reliance on telecommuting and online meetings. And although the technology has been around for years, many small companies had never used it until now. I predict that the increased use of these tools during the pandemic will have an impact on travel and office-space budgets for years to come.

Besides the importance of remaining calm, it is equally important to avoid speculation and to deal instead with known facts. During the first few days of the pandemic, we were inundated with questions for which we had no answers, and it was frustrating. Still, I believe speculation disguised as advice is dangerous during crises, and one of the most reckless things a leader can do is shoot from the hip or play fast and loose with the facts. Just be honest and transparent, and explain what you know.

The best way I've found to respond to questions that do not have definitive answers, whether from a client or an employee, is to start by saying, "We are monitoring events in real time, and here's what we know," then proceed to say what I in fact know to be true. Overpromising but underdelivering during a crisis is the best way to ruin a reputation.

Finally, crisis naturally produces anxiety, and everyone has the same question: "How will this affect me?" It's human nature to worry about events that impact us but over which we have little direct control. We all want reassurance during times of uncertainty, and good leaders will provide that. When I reflect on the many advertisements that have aired during this pandemic, the one phrase that keeps being used over and over is this: "We're all in this together."

That sentiment is meant to strike a warm and unifying tone, and it should reflect how an organization feels about its employees and clients. When circumstances seem to be beyond my control, I choose to focus on what I do control: our core values.

A crisis should not shake your identity as an organization; rather, a crisis should reinforce it. And it should never cause you to lose sight of your mission; rather, it should embolden it. In times of crisis, this is what I emphasize to our people. Our priorities may be temporarily rearranged, and we may even need to adapt new methods of conducting business, but we are undeterred in our mission. The word I've heard most often to describe this pandemic is "unprecedented," and within the span of our lifetime, it certainly is. But there have been pandemics throughout human history. And if the world continues, there will likely be another. In the end, when faced with what appears to be an insurmountable crisis, remember to remain true to your values and mission, and communicate confidence, optimism, and hope.

SITUATIONAL AWARENESS

During any kind of crisis, measuring results on a more-frequent basis is critical for getting through it. Typically, decisive action has been taken at the outset and sometimes before all the facts are known. And since conditions on the ground can change quickly, you must have actionable data to know whether to alter your strategy or to stay the course. Most business owners have some specific Key Performance Indicators (KPIs) they review at regular intervals to keep tabs on how they are doing. At Lyons HR, we review many operational and client-service metrics to measure our own performance. During the COVID-19 crisis, we measured these same metrics weekly, and in some cases, daily. By increasing the frequency of data gathering, we're able to react more quickly to fluctuations that may start to undermine our success.

The importance of situational awareness during a crisis cannot be overstated. Each day, the crisis-management team should seek to answer two questions: how is the crisis evolving, and what impact is it having on our company? The answers to these two questions will shape your strategy. Internal performance metrics are helpful, but the most-telling indicator of how a company is doing during a crisis is learned through client feedback. Are you asking for that feedback? Have you shifted the cost and inconvenience of the crisis to your client, hoping they will understand, or have you created an innovative new approach to ensure client service is not disrupted? Have you discovered a completely new service you can provide to your client, or are you simply focused on what you were doing before? In my experience, I have seen that crises offer opportunity for deeper and more meaningful relationships, particularly if it is a shared crisis, as is the case with COVID-19.

THE SILVER LINING

As we've seen repeatedly, crisis is unavoidable. When it happens, you are either an adapter to that crisis, or you're destroyed and put out of business by that crisis. The small businesses that are able to say, "Here are the challenges, but here's how we're going to modify, to adapt, and to change our behaviors and our service model"—those are the ones that are going to emerge as the real winners.

It may surprise you that many of the most successful companies in the world were started during recessions or other volatile socio-economic circumstances. Here's a list from *Business Insider*[12] of a few company names you may recognize, all of which began during crises:

- General Motors

- Hewlett-Packard

- Burger King

- Hyatt

- Trader Joe's

- Microsoft

- CNN

- Uber

- Airbnb

- Square

- Groupon

PEOs are challenged because of the diversity of the clients we serve. It's not like we're a single-industry service company. We serve

---

12   Matthew Wilson, "14 Successful Companies That Started During US Recessions," *Business Insider*, April 20, 2020, https://www.businessinsider.com/successful-companies-started-during-past-us-recessions-2020-4.

companies that are restaurants; we serve companies that are hotels; we serve companies that are doctors' offices. Among businesses from *A* to *Z* out there, we have clients. So as those businesses change, we must be resourceful by responding and adapting to what happens with them.

The real value of using a PEO is in having a partner who will have your back during difficult and often unforeseen circumstances. PEOs provide their clients with the kind of business continuity of essential services that may be difficult or impossible to maintain on their own. The pandemic was certainly unforeseen, but we understand that our success depends on our clients' success. And because we approach everything from our clients' points of view, we listened, we observed, we learned, we adapted, we innovated, and most importantly, we served.

PEO INDUSTRY SPOTLIGHT

DAN MCHENRY

With more than thirty years of experience in the PEO industry, Dan McHenry has a unique 360-degree view of the industry, as a PEO client, as a PEO executive of what became two of the largest PEOs in the country, and most recently as a PEO consultant. Like many other industry leaders, McHenry has a financial background and started his career as a CPA and CMA, working with an international accounting firm in its Tampa Bay offices. At PricewaterhouseCoopers, McHenry was first hired in the audit department, then took a tour of duty in tax, and ultimately served as the CPS/Emerging Business practice leader, where he focused on the financial and operational aspects of entrepreneurial and emerging businesses. One of the firm's clients was one of the first publicly traded PEOs in the United States. This experience inspired McHenry, at the age of twenty-nine, to form National Business Solutions (NBS) with his partners in the Tampa Bay market, with McHenry serving as the firm's chief financial officer.

"It was an exciting time in the PEO industry, as we were becoming more mainstream as a solution for small businesses. In fact, PEOs had reached such a point of acceptance that we were asking the states to regulate the industry. We felt the industry had matured to the point that the business community needed to know there were consumer protections in place. Arkansas, Florida, and Texas were among the earliest states to pass PEO legislation," McHenry recalled.

Ultimately, NBS was acquired by Paychex to become the origins of its PEO division. After leaving NBS, McHenry partnered with the Wackenhut Corporation to form Oasis Outsourcing in 1996, serving as the company's president and cofounder.

"Those formative years at Oasis were remarkable. Besides helping the small-business community with their human-resource needs, our clients gave us a front-seat view of why small businesses are the engine of the US economy," McHenry said.

In 2002, Wackenhut and Oasis were sold to Group Falck, after which McHenry moved to the service-provider side of the PEO industry. Collaborating with veterans from around the industry, he formed McHenry Consulting, which has since grown to include practice units in business advisory, human-resource strategies, mergers and acquisitions, recruiting, and technology. Working with clients from start-up to publicly traded, the firm advises its clients throughout their businesses' lifecycles. With its reservoir of experience and intellectual capital, the firm's specialty is assisting business owners in maximizing liquidation events at the end of their business journeys and harvesting the fruits of their labor.

In 2017, McHenry and his partners formed White Label HR, which serves as a back-office platform for start-up, early stage, and lifestyle PEOs. This innovative service offers PEOs the infrastructure, guidance, and scalability needed to accelerate profitability. McHenry estimates that between the two firms, he has worked with almost two hundred PEOs, including Lyons HR, and has assisted in the formation, start-up, and launch of over thirty PEOs.

McHenry has been an active member of NAPEO, having served on its Accounting and Finance Committee, Service Provider Committee, and as a contributor to PEO University. He has served as a director for ESAC, has been a frequent speaker at NAPEO conferences, and has authored numerous articles for the *PEO Insider* over the last twenty years. McHenry has served as an adjunct professor for the past twelve years at Florida Atlantic University.

"I have seen the highs and lows of the PEO industry for over thirty years. Before COVID, many have heard me postulate that the industry was at its apex, and that I have never been more bullish on the PEO industry. The impact of COVID has not changed my view," McHenry concluded.

McHenry Consulting is a leading national full-service PEO consulting firm based out of Orlando, Florida.

CHAPTER NINE

PEO INDUSTRY OUTLOOK

Overcoming challenges together makes us stronger partners.

—Bill J. Lyons

J oe feels relief when he thinks about how close he came to laying off some of his talented technicians during the pandemic. Trying to replace them could have been more damaging to his business than dealing with the pandemic itself. Would they have been willing to come back when the federal government was paying an additional $600 per week in unemployment benefits? How long would it have taken him to replace them and get his shop back to full capacity? It had taken twenty-five years to get his shops staffed the way they were, so the thought of starting over gave him a sick feeling.

Would Joe have survived the lockdown without a PEO? Maybe. Could he have navigated the complexity of the CARES Act and maximized his loan proceeds on his own? Again, maybe. Would Joe have been able to provide reassurance to his employees during the lockdown or supply the necessary data to maximize his loan forgiveness? Perhaps he could.

The fact is that partnering with a PEO does not guarantee the success of any business. But statistics prove that a small business's chance of survival is improved by 50 percent if it is with a PEO.[13] Joe is like hundreds of thousands of small-business owners across the country who are wondering what lies ahead in a post-COVID-19 environment. Some may return to a state of being resembling what they were before. But for many, business has been changed forever. Being with a PEO will not guarantee your success, but having a PEO is like having a big brother looking out for you when there is a bully on the playground. Just like Joe's PEO responded to an unprecedented event and took care of him, PEOs all over the country did the same thing for their clients. And when the next unexpected crisis happens, PEOs will be there again to safeguard and to serve their clients.

If I had written this chapter at the end of 2019, it would have likely turned out much differently than what I've written here now. COVID-19 made sure of that. In a nutshell, the outlook for the PEO industry for the 2020s and beyond is just like the outlook of many other industries that are closely tied to economic performance. Recovery and growth will depend on how well the economy responds to the massive shutdowns due to the pandemic. Despite all the fear

---

13 Laurie Bassi and Dan McMurrer, "An Economic Analysis: The PEO Industry Footprint in 2018," *NAPEO White Paper Series* no. 6 (September 2018), https://www.napeo.org/docs/default-source/white-papers/2018-white-paper-final.pdf.

and uncertainty, however, and though the workplace itself will be forever impacted, I think the industry is poised to do well in the post-COVID-19 world.

Let's take a look at some of those impacts and the opportunities that lie ahead.

PEO SUPPORT IN UNCHARTED WATERS

Without a doubt, there will be new and complex requirements for many industries to abide by as we emerge from the shadow of the pandemic. Restaurants have had to make significant modifications to their dining areas to accommodate social distancing guidelines, along with the enhanced hygiene and sanitation standards being mandated. The same sweeping changes have been mandated in the hotel and hospitality industries and in factories, salons, and barbershops across the country—basically anywhere and everywhere employees or customers congregate will be impacted. And like it or not, these new guidelines are going to be with us for quite some time. Since early on in the recovery, PEOs have been called upon by their clients to assist with establishing safe return-to-work protocols. And although the CDC has provided general guidance, each client application has unique characteristics that must be considered when PEOs develop a plan. Bars, restaurants, and nightclubs pose different challenges than those posed by retail stores and professional offices. If there is industry-specific guidance at the state level, this must be taken into consideration, and clearly, enhanced sanitation standards will be necessary in all applications.

Employees may be asked to complete a daily questionnaire to determine whether they have been potentially exposed. And in other cases, state and local authorities are requiring employee temperatures to be taken before an employee is allowed to enter the workplace. In all cases, the employer will need to provide personal protective equipment (PPE) such as masks, gloves, sanitizers, and protective barriers for employees coming in close contact with others. Many professional office settings are closing their lobbies to visitors altogether. The point here is that even though there are general guidelines, no two cases are identical.

As states ease restrictions and as businesses try to reopen, there will undoubtedly be an increase in new litigation if cases again begin to spike. At issue, among other concerns, will be whether the employee contracted COVID-19 at work. How do you prove or disprove that? Another factor will be whether the alleged contraction of the coronavirus occurred in a presumptive state or a nonpresumptive state. Did the employer provide adequate PPE, adhere to enhanced sanitation standards, and comply with all public guidelines from the CDC?

Yes, I believe we will see a flurry of new litigation surrounding COVID-19 that may take years to sort out.

In spite of all the challenges created by COVID-19, clients expect their PEOs to continue delivering all their services without disruption. After all, the four Pillars of Profitability don't get to take time off just because of a pandemic. Now let's consider how COVID-19 will impact the Pillars of Profitability, particularly health insurance and workers' compensation. Where these aspects are concerned, there are huge question marks looming. The government mandated that many of the copays and deductibles associated with coronavirus testing and treatment be waived, which means that insurance companies have had to absorb a higher percentage of the overall medical costs associated with COVID-19. Legislatively, insurance companies are not allowed to charge back for those things, so what effect will this have on the health-insurance industry as a whole, and what kind of pressure will it put on renewal rates?

And what about the workers' compensation claims for essential workers? Workers' compensation is designed to compensate someone for injury or illness sustained during the course of their employment. Frontline workers, delivery drivers, grocery store workers … dozens of new claims roll in every day because of people contracting COVID-19, and this massive explosion in claims is going to have a long-term impact. Some states, such as Illinois, are considered presumptive states under the law, which means that if a person tests positive for COVID-19, it's to be presumed that it was contracted while on the job, making it compensable under workers' compensation law. That essentially shifts the burden of proof from the employee *to* the employer. In those states, we can certainly expect workers' compensation rates to be driven upward. So I believe COVID-19 will result in a hardening of both the health-insurance market, as well as the workers' compensation market in the months and years ahead. And that's going to give most employers fewer choices or make it much more difficult for them to afford quality healthcare for their employees.

The good news for small-business owners who are in relationships with PEOs is that they have teams of experts to rely on for the most up-to-date answers on anything that could potentially affect the livelihood of their businesses in this time of uncertainty. As we saw with Joe's Auto Repair at the opening of this chapter, he was able to navigate all the new laws and regulations to ensure that his business was protected and that his employees and customers remained safe.

Throughout these uncharted waters, larger PEOs will have an advantage over the small boutique and midsize PEOs, because large firms are big enough to negotiate more competitive rates with insurance carriers. This will result in an increase in the current trend of industry consolidation as larger PEOs seek to acquire their midsize competitors. Larger PEOs who are in acquisition mode aren't really interested in small boutique PEOs, however, because these don't represent any significant market share, and that's good news for them. There will always be a role in the market for the small boutique provider that just offers an incredible level of personalized service.

As we move forward in this post-COVID-19 environment, more and more business owners will be looking to their PEOs to help them map out paths forward toward stability, profitability, and growth. The four Pillars of Profitability are going to continue to drive business to the PEO industry just like before. But as we look toward a new normal, there will also be opportunities for wise PEOs to engage new and existing clients.

CRISES CREATE OPPORTUNITIES

Every four years, the NFIB Research Foundation conducts surveys to determine the top concerns of their membership. Their findings are then published in the Small Business Problems and Priorities Report.[14] The most recent report released in June of 2020 revealed these top concerns:

1. Health insurance

2. Locating qualified employees

3. Taxes on business income

4. Retaining skilled employees

5. Government regulations

---

14   Holly Wade and Andrew Heritage, *Small Business Problems and Priorities*, 10th ed. (July 2020), https://assets.nfib.com/nfibcom/NFIB-Problems-and-Priori-ties-2020.pdf.

The rising cost of health insurance has been the number-one concern of small-business owners for the past twenty-nine years, and I expect it will remain the top priority when the 2024 report is released. And although the other priorities may have shifted a place or two, the top five priorities have remained constant. When you consider these top five concerns of small businesses, PEOs currently impact all but one of them. Clearly, PEOs don't influence uncertainty in the economy or the level of federal and state taxation. But PEOs profoundly influence their clients' access to affordable health-insurance options and also help their clients navigate federal and state regulations. PEOs also help their clients reduce federal and state tax liability through strategic benefits-plan design and 401(k)-savings plans. Yet in this post-COVID-19 environment, I believe PEOs will be relied upon more heavily to address concern number two: assisting small businesses in recruitment and professional employee development.

In the past, PEOs have assumed a less-active role in employee recruitment and development. In addition to providing payroll, risk management, and access to benefits, PEOs have historically helped their clients develop effective workplace policies and make sure they were in compliance with all the laws. But that role is about to be expanded.

Even before the pandemic, there was a shortage of qualified employees in certain high-skill positions, and since businesses have reopened, the problem has gotten worse. At the time of this writing, some companies are being forced to operate with less than ideal staffing, simply because they can't find the right people. Recruiting sites like ZipRecruiter and Indeed are helpful tools, but the most-qualified talent is usually not looking for a job. This is where PEOs can step up and fill a large void for their clients, and the ones that do will be rewarded with increased business and client loyalty. Also, the development of retention strategies that include professional development for employees is going to be a hot trend in the years following COVID-19. And with alternative work arrangements emerging as a part of the new normal, PEOs will be able to further serve their clients by advising on and helping to implement remote-work strategies.

> **The reality is that clients are going to be demanding more from their PEOs now and in the future than they ever have before. Wise PEOs will seize this opportunity and embrace these changes, which will make them indispensable to the small businesses they serve.**

The reality is that clients are going to be demanding more from their PEOs now and in the future than they ever have before. Wise PEOs will seize this opportunity and embrace these changes, which will make them indispensable to the small businesses they serve.

THE ROAD AHEAD

From a thirty-thousand-foot view, I believe the PEO industry will continue to grow, but at a slower rate than it has over the past two or three years. We're going to continue to see consolidation of the more than nine hundred PEOs and fewer new entries into the market, because the licensing and capital requirements to get into the PEO business are getting more and more prohibitive. Growth in the PEO industry has historically followed this trend, since this is the segment of the economy that we serve.[15] I see a flattening in terms of the number of new PEOs that enter into the business, with the exception of companies that wish to diversify their services. For example, large insurance brokers who have fifty thousand or more clients often compete and lose business to PEOs. In this new climate, they may well decide to just start their own PEO arm, because they are well-funded and already have a built-in relationship with potential clients. Those are the kind of large entries that I think we're going to see coming into the industry in the early 2020s.

One thing that we'll all be watching for are new amendments to insurance policies, and an increase in premiums to match, regarding some kind of fixed pandemic-insurance provision. The insurance industry took a big hit when the terrorist attacks of 9/11 happened, as most policies didn't include a terrorism-risk component. Now every general liability and property policy has a terrorism-risk premium added to it, and you can expect a similar pandemic premium to be added in the future.

It's going to be more important than ever on the road ahead for small businesses that want to grow and thrive to view human resources as a strategic initiative, as opposed to something they have to do to pay people. Wise business owners view HR as strategic, not transactional, and that's why the title of this book is *We Are HR*. PEOs help business owners develop a plan so they can leverage their human-resource strategies to improve profitability.

We help our clients adapt to changing conditions in the workplace. And if there's one thing that we've all learned in 2020, it's that conditions can change very quickly. Legislation from the federal and the state levels can come at a small-business owner like Joe at a speed that makes it almost impossible to interpret. If you don't have

---

15   Ibid.

people who are watching out for you—experts who can help you and guide you through it—you can and will get lost.

I can almost guarantee with some degree of certainty that on or about the year 2030, we're going to be faced with a different crisis. Like I mentioned in chapter eight, every ten years or so it seems like there is a major reset in the economy. And one of the most important values that PEOs bring to their clients is helping them adapt to survive when conditions change rapidly.

ASOs, as well as cloud-based payroll platforms that claim their software can do everything, are not going away. In fact, new ones are likely going to pop up regularly as an alternative to PEOs. But make no mistake about it: the PEO industry will continue to grow and thrive as more small-business owners come to understand the benefits of coemployment—the ability to share employer liabilities, to gain access to better and more-affordable benefits options due to economies of scale, and to enjoy the support of a dedicated team of subject-matter experts that always have your back. Nowhere else, other than in a PEO relationship, can a small-business owner get all this value.

Starting and running a small business is tough. It has its own risks and rewards every single day, even under normal conditions. If you couple this with a crisis every ten years or so, it just makes a lot of sense to be in a PEO relationship. Nowhere else can you insulate your company from all that can go wrong while realizing the potential for growth. The fact is that most small businesses that do not use a PEO don't have any kind of HR expertise on staff.

Think back to when you started your business. If you are like most entrepreneurs, you had a great idea, or you started your business out of necessity; or maybe you just wanted to be your own boss. But now, if you are like the typical small-business owner, you're spending as much as 30 percent of your time on employment-related issues, an average of over two hours each day. What could you do with that time if you had it back? Would you spend it developing new products or services, opening new markets, or acquiring new customers? Maybe you would just spend more time with your family or go watch your son's Little League baseball game. Whatever it is, we know you didn't start your business so you could be an employer. But that's why we exist.

That's why *We ARE HR*.

A P P E N D I X

I. LABOR LAWS AFFECTING THE PEO INDUSTRY

Acronym	Act	EE Threshold	Year Passed	Governed By
Title VII	Civil Rights Act	15	1964	EEOC
ADA	Americans with Disabilities Act	15	1990	EEOC
FMLA	Family & Medical Leave Act	50/10	1993	DOL
ADEA	Age Discrimination in Employment Act	20	1967	EEOC
IRCA	Immigration Reform & Control Act	0	1986	DHSA
USERRA	Uniformed Services Employment & Reemployment Rights Act	0	1994	DOL

OSHA	Occupational Safety & Health Act	1	1970	OSHA
COBRA	Consolidated Omnibus Budget Reconciliation Act	20	1985	DOL
HIPAA	Health Insurance Portability & Accountability Act	1	1996	DOL
ERISA	Employee Retirement Income Security Act	All	1974	DOL
FLSA	Fair Labor Standards Act	All	1938	DOL W&H
PRWORA	Personal Responsibility Work Opportunity Reconciliation Act	0	1996	OCSE
EPPA	Employee Polygraph Protection Act	0	1988	DOL

II. SBEA FLOW CHART

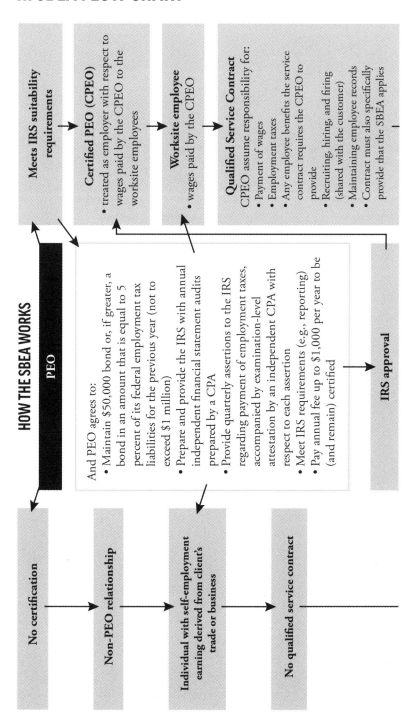

HOW THE SBEA WORKS

PEO

Meets IRS suitability requirements

Certified PEO (CPEO)
• treated as employer with respect to wages paid by the CPEO to the worksite employees

Worksite employee
• wages paid by the CPEO

Qualified Service Contract
CPEO assume responsibility for:
• Payment of wages
• Employment taxes
• Any employee benefits the service contract requires the CPEO to provide
• Recruiting, hiring, and firing (shared with the customer)
• Maintaining employee records
• Contract must also specifically provide that the SBEA applies

And PEO agrees to:
• Maintain $50,000 bond or, if greater, a bond in an amount that is equal to 5 percent of its federal employment tax liabilities for the previous year (not to exceed $1 million)
• Prepare and provide the IRS with annual independent financial statement audits prepared by a CPA
• Provide quarterly assertions to the IRS regarding payment of employment taxes, accompanied by examination-level attestation by an independent CPA with respect to each assertion
• Meet IRS requirements (e.g., reporting)
• Pay annual fee up to $1,000 per year to be (and remain) certified

IRS approval

No certification

Non-PEO relationship

Individual with self-employment earning derived from client's trade or business

No qualified service contract

Qualifying worksite
- At least 85 percent of the individuals performing services for the customer at the worksite must be subject to one or more qualifying service contracts with the CPEO.

CPEO

And PEO agrees to:
- Has clear statutory authority to collect and remit federal employment taxes under its EIN for wages it pays to worksite employees
- The FICA and FUTA wage bases will not restart when a customer joins or leaves the CPEO mid-year
- Customers of CPEOs will qualify for specified federal tax credits that the customers would be entitled to claim if there were no PEO relationship
- If a CPEO (or a customer) makes a contribution to a state unemployment fun with respect to wages paid to a worksite employee, the CPEO receives the federal (FUTA) tax credit with respect to that contribution

If less than 85 percent of individuals at the customer worksite are not subject to the qualifying service contract, certain workers may not be counted:
- Collectively bargained employees
- Employees with fewer than six months of service
- Employees who work fewer than 17.5 hours per week
- Certain seasonal employees
- Employees under age 21

Current law

III. STATES AND THEIR LICENSING REQUIREMENTS

State	PEO Registration Required	Type of Registration	Regulating Agency	Audited Financials Required	Minimum Net Worth Required	Minimum Working Capital Required
Alabama	Yes	Registration	Department of Labor	Yes	$100,000	No
Alaska	No	N/A	—	—	—	No
Arizona	No	N/A	—	—	—	No
Arkansas	Yes	Licensing	Department of Insurance	Yes	$100,000	No
California	Yes	Registration	Department of Industrial Relations	—	—	No
Colorado	Yes	Certification	Department of Labor & Employment	Yes	—	$100,000

State	PEO Registration Required	Type of Registration	Regulating Agency	Audited Financials Required	Minimum Net Worth Required	Minimum Working Capital Required
Connecticut	Yes	Registration	Department of Labor	Yes	—	$150,000
Delaware	No	N/A	—	—	—	No
Florida	Yes	Licensing	Department of Business & Professional Regulation	Yes	$50,000	Yes
Georgia	No	N/A	—	—	—	No
Hawaii	Yes	Registration	Department of Industrial Relations	—	—	No
Idaho	No	N/A	Department of Labor	—	—	No

State	PEO Registration Required	Type of Registration	Regulating Agency	Audited Financials Required	Minimum Net Worth Required	Minimum Working Capital Required
Illinois	Yes	Registration	Department of Insurance	—	—	No
Indiana	Yes	Registration	Department of Insurance	Yes	—	$100,000
Iowa	No	N/A	Department of Workforce Development	—	—	No
Kansas	Yes	Registration	Department of Insurance	Yes	—	Yes
Kentucky	Yes	Registration	Department of Workers' Claims	—	—	No
Louisiana	Yes	Registration	Department of Insurance	—	—	No

State	PEO Registration Required	Type of Registration	Regulating Agency	Audited Financials Required	Minimum Net Worth Required	Minimum Working Capital Required
Maine	Yes	Registration	Department of Professional & Financial Regulation	—	—	No
Maryland	No	N/A	—	—	—	No
Massachusetts	Yes	Registration	Department of Labor & Workforce Development	Yes	—	Yes
Michigan	Yes	Licensing	Department of Licensing & Regulatory Affairs	Yes	—	$100,000
Minnesota	Yes	Registration	Department of Commerce	—	—	No
Mississippi	No	N/A	—	—	—	No

State	PEO Registration Required	Type of Registration	Regulating Agency	Audited Financials Required	Minimum Net Worth Required	Minimum Working Capital Required
Missouri	Yes	Registration	Secretary of State	Yes	—	$100,000
Montana	Yes	Licensing	Department of Labor & Industry	Yes	$50,000	Yes
Nebraska	Yes	Registration	Department of Labor	Yes	—	$100,000
Nevada	Yes	Registration	Department of Business & Industry	Yes	—	Yes
New Hampshire	Yes	Licensing	Department of Labor	Yes	—	$100,000
New Jersey	Yes	Registration	Department of Labor & Workforce Development	Yes	—	$100,000

State	PEO Registration Required	Type of Registration	Regulating Agency	Audited Financials Required	Minimum Net Worth Required	Minimum Working Capital Required
New Mexico	Yes	Registration	Department of Regulation & Licensing	—	—	No
New York	Yes	Registration	Department of Labor	Yes	$75,000	No
North Carolina	Yes	Licensing	Department of Insurance	Yes	—	Yes
North Dakota	Yes	Licensing	Secretary of State	—	—	No
Ohio	Yes	Registration	Bureau of Workers' Compensation	Yes	—	$1
Oklahoma	Yes	Registration	Department of Insurance	Yes	—	No

State	PEO Registration Required	Type of Registration	Regulating Agency	Audited Financials Required	Minimum Net Worth Required	Minimum Working Capital Required
Oregon	Yes	Licensing	Department of Consumer & Business Services	—	—	No
Pennsylvania	Yes	N/A	—	—	—	No
Rhode Island	Yes	Registration	Department of Revenue	—	—	No
South Carolina	Yes	Licensing	Department of Consumer Affairs	Yes	—	$1
South Dakota	No	N/A	—	—	—	No
Tennessee	Yes	Licensing	Department of Commerce & Insurance	Yes	—	$1

State	PEO Registration Required	Type of Registration	Regulating Agency	Audited Financials Required	Minimum Net Worth Required	Minimum Working Capital Required
Texas	Yes	Licensing	Department of Licensing & Regulation	Yes	—	$50,000
Utah	Yes	Licensing	Department of Insurance	Yes	—	$100,000
Vermont	Yes	Licensing	Department of Labor	Yes	$100,000	No
Virginia	Yes	Registration	Workers' Compensation Commission	—	—	No
Washington	No	N/A	—	—	—	No
Washington DC	No	N/A	—	—	—	No

State	PEO Registration Required	Type of Registration	Regulating Agency	Audited Financials Required	Minimum Net Worth Required	Minimum Working Capital Required
West Virginia	Yes	Licensing	Office of the Insurance Commissioner	Yes	—	$100,000
Wisconsin	Yes	Registration	Department of Financial Institutions	Yes	—	$100,000
Wyoming	No	N/A	—	—	—	No